Pheasant Breeding
and Care

Fifth Edition,
Revised and Expanded

by Dr. Jean Delacour

Color photos in this book taken by D.R. Baylis, Berkshire, England except those on pages 40, 44, 48, 49, 80, 116, 125. Color photos, pages 116 and 125 by Horst Muller.

0·87666·969·0

-0. MAR 1986

ISBN 0-87666-969-0

Distributed in the U.S.A. by T.F.H. Publications, Inc., 211 West Sylvania Avenue, P.O. Box 27, Neptune City, N.J. 07753; in England by T.F.H. (Gt. Britain) Ltd., 13 Nutley Lane, Reigate, Surrey; in Canada to the book store and library trade by Clarke, Irwin & Company, Clarwin House, 791 St. Clair Avenue West, Toronto 10, Ontario; in Canada to the pet trade by Rolf C. Hagen Ltd., 3225 Sartelon Street, Montreal 382, Quebec; in Southeast Asia by Y.W. Ong, 9 Lorong 36 Geylang, Singapore 14; in Australia and the south Pacific by Pet Imports Pty. Ltd., P.O. Box 149, Brookvale 2100, N.S.W., Australia. Published by T.F.H. Publications Inc., Ltd., The British Crown Colony of Hong Kong.

Table of Contents

In Support of Conservation

A third of the species that are described in this book are currently listed as endangered. Urgent action is required *now* if these valuable and spectacular birds are to be preserved for future generations to see and enjoy.

In keeping with his desire for the conservation of these species, Dr. Jean Delacour, author of this book and president of the World Pheasant Association, urges adherence to the goals of his organization.

The World Pheasant Association aims to develop, promote and support conservation of all species of the order *Galliformes* with initial emphasis on the family *Phasianidae* by:

1) Encouraging sound and improved methods of aviculture, both in the countries of origin and elsewhere in the world.

2) Establishing a data-bank for the *Galliformes* and acting as an advisory body to the members of the Association and to outside organizations on all matters relating to the ecology, conservation, protection and breeding of these birds.

3) Promoting constructive research in the wild and through aviculture and publishing the results in the interests of conservation.

4) Educating the public by all means to a better appreciation of *Galliformes* in particular and nature in general.

5) Establishing reserve collections and buffer stocks of threatened or endangered species under the surveillance of the Association and in collaboration with the governments of the countries of origin and approved breeders.

Preface

CHARLES F. DENLEY was for many years the most enthusiastic and successful breeder of pheasants in the United States. Bird-keeping was entirely a hobby with him, and it was for his own pleasure and interest that he gathered an outstanding collection which he kept in excellent condition, rearing a number of young every year. He probably has done more than anyone else in his time to promote interest in pheasants in the Western World. I knew him well and greatly appreciated his vast knowledge of the birds and his genuine personality.

Denley's *Ornamental Pheasants, Their Breeding and Care* is a brief and condensed but excellent account of his own experiences and methods. It has been out of print for too long, but it is a most useful handbook.

Detailed information on all the pheasants, adequately illustrated, will be found in my book *The Pheasants of the World,* but a book specifically on the practical aspects of the subject is a necessity for experienced breeders and sportsmen as well as beginners. Therefore I have revised and brought up to date the work of my late friend.

The fourth edition of this work came out more than twenty years ago, and a great deal of information has recently become available. Although only one new subspecies (*Lophura nycthemera omeiensis*, a Silver Pheasant from western China with almost pure black side tail feathers) has been discovered during that time, we have learned much of the life habits, behavior and breeding of so far little known species which have reached and been bred in American and European aviaries during the last twenty years.

OPPOSITE:
Germain's Peacock Pheasant *(Polyplectron germaini)*

7

New methods and ways of feeding and rearing game birds have developed as a result of new research and experiments with prepared foods, incubators and brooders. These new techniques have made things easier and simpler, a necessity because of today's scarcity and high cost of skilled labor. They also have proved safer, avoiding chances of contagion in many cases. Yet Charles Denley's advice remains sound, and little has had to be added to his recommendations.

J. Delacour, New York, 1977

Introduction

In this work on the care and breeding of ornamental pheasants, it is the writer's desire to lead the amateur step by step from the egg to the adult bird. No claim is made that this is the correct and only method of breeding pheasants, but it is the method developed at my establishment, Winden, and it has been successful in the case of every species of bird that has come under the writer's hand, which includes thirty-odd species of pheasants.

There are probably as many methods of raising pheasants as there are breeders. Naturally, some methods are better than others, and all are more or less successful. My method is not perfect and, as time goes on, I expect to improve it. In retrospect, it is a great satisfaction to see the improvement that has taken place in the past thirty years. Game breeding is no longer a mystery; no longer is the closely guarded secret handed down only from father to son, for today the young of the rare and expensive species are raised on mash that can be bought for three cents a pound.

It has been the writer's experience that men breeding pheasants for profit are not inclined to speak freely of their methods, preferring to keep to themselves what they have learned, in order to keep a jump or two ahead of the other fellow. This is not the policy of this writer. Pheasants are his hobby, and it is his earnest desire to aid others by disseminating the best available information, founded on personal experience.

The country home can have no greater attraction than a collection of fancy pheasants. Taken as a whole, pheasants are more adapted to life in captivity than any other group of birds. Included in the pheasant family are our common chickens, peafowl and turkeys—certainly pheasants are no more difficult to breed, considering their unadvanced stage of domestication. Their eggs and flesh are a source of one of the most valuable and dependable foods that nature has provided. For brilliancy of color and elaborateness of feather ornaments pheasants are equalled by only one other group: the hummingbirds.

It is regrettable that Americans have been so backward about taking up the breeding of fancy pheasants. The success of game breeders who have undertaken the breeding of the Ringneck for sporting purposes has been most remarkable. The small breeder cannot compete with the large producer, who sells annually thousands of birds and eggs, but he can profitably breed the fancy species, as it requires no more food or labor to raise a bird worth $100 than one worth $5.00.

It is my earnest belief that if the bird-loving public should acquire a better knowledge of pheasants and become better acquainted with their wonderful beauty and hardiness and the trifling amount of food they require, this beautiful family of exotic birds would come into their own and become the most abundantly bred family of birds in the world.

Most species of pheasants have constitutions hardy enough to stand our severest northern winters not more than a good windbreak. Those species, however, that inhabit the tropical jungles have not yet been acclimated to the point where they can stand our cold weather without artificial heat.

So many varieties of pheasants are available that there is a size and color to please almost everyone—from the fourteen-ounce female of the Golden and Germain's Peacock Pheasant to the seven-pound Impeyan male, and the most wonderful of all: the giant Argus. And they are no more expensive than many of our fancy breeds of poultry.

In the following pages I submit the results of my thirty-three years' experience in pheasant breeding. These results I have endeavored to render as clearly and simply as possible. If, as a result of my efforts, the number of pheasants in America is increased by only a few pairs, I shall feel amply rewarded.

Charles F. Denley
Glenmount, Maryland, U.S.A.
1935

OPPOSITE:
Berlioz Pheasant *(Lophura berliozi)*

The Pheasant Groups and Species

One calls pheasants the large game birds of the Old World, the males of which have an ornamental and elaborate plumage and unfeathered legs. Their very close relatives, the partridges and the quails, are very similar, only smaller as a rule, and less brightly colored; the grouse and guinea fowls are slightly more different, and the turkeys still more different.

There are sixteen distinct groups, or genera, of pheasants which include the Junglefowls, ancestors of domestic poultry, the Argus and the Peafowls. All are found in Asia, with the exception of one which lives in Africa's Congo region. There are 175 different kinds (species and subspecies) in the sixteen genera.

All of the pheasants, with very few exceptions, live and breed well in captivity. A number have adapted themselves to new climates and are established in American and European aviaries, while others are more or less uncommon, and a few are even rare.

It is very likely that a number of pheasants will sooner or later become extinct as their habitat is gradually penetrated by human beings and destroyed. It therefore becomes very important for the conservation of many beautiful species to propagate them in captivity.

BLOOD PHEASANTS

The Blood Pheasants (genus *Ithaginis*) inhabit the high mountains of China, Burma and India. The cocks are beautifully colored in gray, pale green and crimson; they are crested, their feathers are lance-shaped and they have a short tail. They are

OPPOSITE:
Peafowl *(Pavo muticus)*

small; females are brown. They are difficult to keep in captivity, as they are very susceptible to infection at low altitudes. Very few have been imported, and none had been bred in America or in Europe until a few years ago.

They all belong to one species, *Ithaginis cruentus,* which varies a great deal according to distribution and includes fifteen sub-species, varying in the amount of red and green in the plumage of the males.

TRAGOPANS

The Tragopans (genus *Tragopan*) also live at high altitudes in the forests of India, Burma and China, in a damp and often chilly climate. But they do well in captivity if given plenty of space and a diet mostly of fruit and green food; they eat leaves avidly. They are hardy but dislike great heat and strong sun. The cocks are beautifully spotted on a red, gray or buff background, and they have highly colored skin ornaments on the head and throat. During the breeding season, they spread out a large bib of brightly colored skin with an extraordinary pattern. Females are brown and speckled. They are tame and gentle, and very handsome; most desirable, but not easy to keep in warm weather.

Tragopans' pens should be roomy enough to allow plenty of exercise, at least twelve by thirty feet, with lots of trees and bushes for shade and for perches, as they roost a great deal, even in daytime. In a large pen two hens can be kept with one cock. Nests (baskets or boxes) should be hung high, as Tragopan hens dislike laying on the ground. They breed in their second year.

There are five species: Western Tragopan (very rare); Satyr Tragopan; Temminck's Tragopan; Blyth's Tragopan (rare); and Cabot's Tragopan. All have been bred in captivity.

The **Satyr Tragopan** *(Tragopan satyra)* the largest species, is from the Himalayas. The cock has a black head, deep crimson underparts spotted with black and pale gray, brown upperparts, also spotted, and a short spur on each leg. First year males are

OPPOSITE:
Temminck's Tragopan *(Tragopan temmincki)*

14

brown, buff and black, very much smaller than males. Eggs, buff spotted with reddish, five or six in a clutch; incubation: 28 days.

Temminck's Tragopan (*Tragopan temmincki*) is smaller than the Satyr, the head with more red and the blue skin more apparent; underparts light red with large, pale gray spots; upperparts darker red with smaller spots. Young cocks and females much like Satyrs, but smaller and grayer. Comes from the mountains of western China. The most easily kept Tragopan in captivity.

Cabot's Tragopan (*Tragopan caboti*), from the mountains of eastern China, used to be also numerous in captivity and bred freely. It requires, however, plenty of space and shade, as the males are particularly subject to strokes if confined too closely. It is rather a small bird, plain buff below, spotted buff, red and black above, with the crown and neck red and black, the face and throat orange. Female is grayer than Temminck's. There are now only a few pairs in America and in Europe.

Himalayan Monal and female (right) (*Lophophorus impeyanus*)

Blyth's Tragopan (*Tragopan blythi*), from Assam and Burma, has a black crown and red neck; face and throat golden yellow; resembles Temminck's above, but gray below. A large bird, found in European aviaries before the war.

The **Western Tragopan** (*Tragopan melanocephalus*), from Kashmir, is dark gray spotted with white above, the head black, the face and throat scarlet, the neck and upper breast red; underparts spotted black and white. It is difficult to maintain and to breed, and it has seldom been imported.

KOKLASS

The Koklass (genus *Pucrasia*) are also mountain birds of China and India; they have sober plumage, but a long crest, arrow-shaped feathers and a delicate pattern of brown, chestnut, gray and black. Female, brown and laced. Difficult to keep in many districts; susceptible to infection; requires a diet of greens and vegetables, with little grain. There are ten different kinds, all much alike. While they do very well at certain times and in certain places, they disappear quickly from others. Perhaps a better technique will help in keeping and propagating these fine birds more easily. There is but one species, with ten well-marked subspecies, three of which have been imported and reared: the **Common** (*P. m. macrolopha*), **Yellow-necked** (*P. m. xanthospila*) and **Darwin's** (*P. m. darwini*).

MONALS

The Monals (genus *Lophophorus*) form another group of highland birds found in Northern India and in China. Large, heavy-crested birds, the cocks have an extraordinarily shiny metallic blue, green and purple plumage. Females brown, streaked with white. There are three species, but only one bred in captivity (*Himalayan Monal*, also called *Impeyan Monal*). They breed in their second year.

Impeyan Monal (*Lophophorus impeyanus*) is found all along the Himalayas at high altitudes. Completely hardy; a large stocky bird with a short, square tail. The cock is velvety black below, brilliantly metallic blue and purple above; lower back white; tail reddish cinnamon; head crested, green; neck blue and purple; upperback golden green. Female a mottled brown, black and white with a very short crest and a white throat. First year males look like females, but are larger and have a few black feathers on the throat. Eggs, ruddy buff and spotted, four to six in a clutch; incubation: 27 days.

Impeyans dig constantly; they need ample room and a dry sandy or rocky soil. They can stand any degree of cold, but fear dampness. Must be kept in pairs.

The other two Monals, **Sclater's** (*L. sclateri*) and **Chinese** (*L. lhuysi*), are also very beautiful and have similar metallic colors. They are extremely rare and have only rarely been kept in captivity; so far they never have bred.

JUNGLEFOWL

The Junglefowl (genus *Gallus*) consist of four species native to the warm parts of Ceylon, India, Burma, Indo-China and Malaysia. The **Red Junglefowl** is the ancestor of domestic poultry and looks like a slender red and black bantam. But the comb is small and the tail held almost horizontally. In the summer, after the molt, the neck and side hackles are lost, and the cock shows a thin black neck for a couple of months. The Red Junglefowl *(Gallus gallus)* has five subspecies.

Silver Pheasant *(Lophura nycthemera)*

The other three species—the Gray, the Ceylon and the Green—are exceedingly beautiful, the first two fairly hardy and easy to rear, the last more delicate.

Ceylon Junglefowl (*Gallus lafayettei*). The cock has a dented red comb with a large yellow patch in the middle. It is fiery orange, lined with black, the wings and tail bright purple; yellow legs. The hen has a pale breast and strong barring on the wings. It is hardy and easy to keep, breeding freely, but only in the second year.

Gray Junglefowl (*Gallus sonnerati*). The dented red comb of the cock resembles that of the Red Junglefowl; it has laced gray and black mantle and underparts and bronzy black wings and tail, but its principal adornments are the horny yellow spangles of the ruff and wing coverts; pink legs. The female has white underparts, laced with black. Easy to keep and to rear. It comes from western and southern India. This bird is also called Sonnerat's Junglefowl.

Green Junglefowl (*Gallus varius*). A more different bird, the cock with bright blue, green and yellow patches in the comb, which is not dented; its upper plumage metallic green, feathers laced with black, yellow and red lines and spots on the wings and rump. Hen laced above. Lives in the dryer parts of Java and the Lesser Sunda Islands. It is susceptible to cold and dampness and the chicks are delicate. It is not suitable for cold countries. Also called Java Jungle Fowl.

GALLOPHEASANTS

The Gallopheasants (genus *Lophura*) include many species; the most popular are the Silvers, the Kalijs and the Firebacks. All are very easy to rear. They lay eight to fifteen eggs; incubation is 25 days as a rule. They all possess large face wattles, a crest, and a curved tail.

Silvers

The Silver group is white streaked with black above, black below; red legs. They come from Siam, Indo-China and southern China and there a number of different subspecies, darker in the South and lighter in the North; the best known being the true Silver and the Berlioz. Breed the second year, occasionally the first.

Silver Pheasant (*L. nycthemera*). A large species, the cock with a long white tail. Face crimson; long black crest; upperparts white, finely lined with black; bill yellow; legs crimson. First year males brown, larger and lighter than females, the breast and the tail with more bars. Female earthy brown, more or less streaked with whitish below. Lives in southern China and Tonkin. The easiest ornamental pheasant to keep and breed. Several hens can be kept with one cock; it does well at liberty, although it is a poor game bird as it seldom flies.

Berlioz Pheasant (*L. berliozi*). Resembles the Silver, but tail shorter and upperparts darker, the black streaks wider and more numerous. Found in northern Annam. Scarce in pheasantries, but hardy and easy to keep.

Kalijs

The *Black Kalij* group from northern India and Burma has a shorter tail and the body is mostly black, with white markings, legs gray; some are common in captivity, hardy and very easy to care for, but pugnacious and better kept in pairs. Males take their plumage the first year; breed also the first year.

White-crested Kalij (*L. hamiltoni*). From the western Himalayas; has a long white or gray crest and a rather short tail. Cock bluish-black with pale brown borders to the feathers; breast and rump striped and barred, mostly white; legs gray. The female is mottled brown and gray, rather pale, with a long crest; central tail feathers blackish.

Nepal Kalij (*L. leucomelana*). Similar, but with a black crest and less white on breast and rump. Female browner.

Black-backed Kalij (*L. melanota*). Differs only in the rump being entirely black. Lives in Sikkim and Bhutan. Female dark and reddish.

Black-breasted Kalij (*L. lathami*). (Also called **Horsfield's Kalij**.) Tail shorter, legs higher; crest more upstanding, breast black, but rump lined with white. Female differs from others in having chestnut central tail feathers instead of black. Comes from Assam and northern Burma.

Lineated Kalij (*L. lineata*). From South Burma; cock very finely streaked black and white above, looking gray; black below. Hen brown with sharp black and white markings on breast and back. A pretty bird, quite distinct.

Nepal Kalij *(Lophura leucomelana)*

The *Blue Kalij* group cocks have a shorter crest, the female none; red legs. Keep in pairs; breed in second year.

Imperial Pheasant (*L. imperialis*). A very rare bird from northern Annam. Cock entirely dark blue; female light brown. First year cocks have much brown in plumage. Hardy and easy to keep, but inbred, as only one wild pair ever captured (1923).

Edwards's Pheasant *(L. edwardsi)*. Smaller, blue with green markings on the shoulders and a white crest, short tail. Female, uniform brown. First year cocks like adults. Comes from central Annam; imported in 1924. Hardy and beautiful, suitable for small pens.

Swinhoe's Pheasant (*L. swinhoei*). A large bird, with a long tail. Cock blue, with white crest, upper back and central tail feathers; shoulders maroon and green. Hen finely mottled chestnut and black. First year males brown and black. A beautiful species from Formosa, long reared in captivity, hardy and strong. Often breeds the first year in captivity.

Salvadori's Pheasant (*L. inornata*). A rare Sumatran species, has lived in captivity only once (France) before 1940. There are a

Bornean Crested Fireback (*Lophura ignita*)

few now in American and European pheasantries, and chicks have been reared since 1976. The cock is crestless, dark purplish blue, the female chestnut; both with a short, square tail.

Firebacks

The Fireback group is composed of large birds with a fairly short tail and long legs; always a coppery red or yellow patch on the lower back in the males. They inhabit the warmer parts of Indo-China and Malaysia and are not hardy in cold countries, requiring a shelter and some heat in the winter. They are bad-tempered and must be kept in pairs.

The **Siamese Fireback** (*L. diardi*). From Indo-China, a hardy bird. The cock is very elegant, gray and purplish black, with a yellow back, elaborate markings, and a long crest hanging on the nape, face crimson. Female crestless; chestnut, brown and black. It is a tame species, breeding well, but only in its third year, while all the other Gallopheasants so far mentioned breed in their first or second year. Requires heat in very cold sections only.

The **Crestless Firebacks** (*L. erythrophthalma*). Seldom kept. The cocks are dark gray, streaked with white, with a red back and a short buff tail the shape of a domestic hen's. Females entirely black. Come from Sumatra and Borneo. Those from the latter country (*L.e. pyronota*) are a lighter gray.

The *Crested Firebacks* form a group of very large dark blue birds, some with chestnut underparts and white or buff in the tail. Short and broad crests. Face wattles light blue. Females chestnut. Satisfactory only in the warmer districts. Cannot stand frost.

Malay Crested Fireback (*L. rufa*). A bulky, dark blue bird, with white central tail feathers and streaks on the sides; legs red. Lives in Malaya, Sumatra.

Bornean Crested Fireback (*L. ignita*). Similar, but less heavy in shape, the belly dark chestnut, the central tail feathers cinnamon and the legs whitish. Female a lighter chestnut. A native of Borneo.

Bulwer's Pheasant (*L. bulweri*). The most beautiful species, has seldom been bred in captivity. It is blue and purple, with an enormous white tail and large blue facial wattles. A few have been reared in the United States and in Mexico, for the first time in 1975. But it is not easy to propagate them.

EARED PHEASANTS

Eared Pheasants (genus *Crossoptilon*) are found high up in the cold parts of northwestern China and in Tibet. Alone among pheasants, the sexes are alike, the cock differing only in its larger size, in the higher and stronger red legs, with a spur (which is not always present), and in the rounder, less oval red wattles of the face. Usually breed the second year.

There are three species: the Brown (also called *Manchurian*), Blue and White. All very handsome, with a long and fluffy tail and hairlike feathers. Tame and amusing, very hardy and easy to breed. Need plenty of room, as they dig a lot. Should be kept in pairs. Require lots of greens, grass and roots, otherwise they will eat one another's feathers.

Blue Eared Pheasant (*Crossoptilon auritum*). Gray blue, with a black cap and long white "ears"; tail black, with a large white patch. Lives in northwest China; imported in 1929 only. Breeds easily and completely hardy. Cocks often eat eggs, which are plain grayish brown; incubation 26-28 days.

Brown Eared Pheasant (*C. mantchuricum*). Similar in shape to the Blue, but tail not quite so finely composed. Body purplish brown; tail white with black tip. Introduced early (1864) into Europe and reared ever since, never having been imported again. From northern China; probably extinct in the wild state.

White Eared Pheasant (*C. crossoptilon*). A heavier bird with a flatter, thicker tail and short "ears." White, with black cap and tail; pale gray wings. Comes from western China and Tibet.

There are several subspecies, varying in color from almost pure white (*C.c. drouyni*) to dark blue (*C.c. harmani*), always easily distinguished from the other two species by their much shorter "ears" and thicker, flatter tails. Rare in captivity. A few specimens came to California twenty-five years ago and some have been reared since, but the species has remained scarce in pheasantries. They belong to the gray-winged subspecies (*C.c. crossoptilon*). More recently, a good many have been raised in Europe and in America, mostly of the white race *C.c. drouyni.*

CHEER

Cheer *(Catreus wallichi).* A curious pheasant, rather dully colored, streaked with brown, buff, gray and black; has a long crest and tail. Female almost like the male. Lives in the Himalayas. Great diggers, fearing dampness. Tame, hardy and easy to rear if kept away from mud and humidity.

LONG-TAILED PHEASANTS

The Long-Tailed Pheasants (genus *Syrmaticus*) include five mountain species from Japan, Burma, Formosa and China; all very beautiful, with long narrow tails, but bad tempered.

Reeves' Pheasant (*S. reevesi*). From central and western China. A large, fine bird. Cocks have tremendously long tail; head and neck white, with a black band from bill to nape; body color

OPPOSITE:
Brown Eared Pheasant *(Crossoptilon mantchuricum)*

Left: Indian Peafowl
(Pavo cristatus)

Above: Soemmerring's Pheasant (*Phasianus soemmerringi*). **Right:** Siamese Fireback (*Lophura diardi*), female. **Below:** Green Peafowl (*Pavo muticus*)

yellow and well-marked with buff, brown, gray and black. A strong and hardy species. It is better to keep two or three hens with one cock. Suitable game birds to introduce into forested and hilly country. Eggs olive brown, seven to fifteen; incubation 24-25 days. Breeds the first year.

Elliot's Pheasant (*S. ellioti*). From eastern China; another fine species, to be treated like Reeves, but not quite so hardy. The cock has a pale gray head and neck, with black face, barred on foreneck; breast and mantle coppery red; belly white: back laced black and white; tail, barred red and pale gray. Female brown, well marked with chestnut and black. Eggs, rosy white, six to eight; incubation 25 days. Breeds usually the second year.

Mikado Pheasant (*S. mikado*). From Formosa; a scarce species. Cock dark blue, with shiny green borders on the shoulders; wings, rump and tail barred with white. Female, earthy brown with white and black markings. Introduced in 1912. Hardy and fairly easy to rear. Eggs, large, creamy white, five to ten; incubation 27-28 days. A cock will do for several hens. Breeds the second year.

Coppers *(S. soemmerringi)* are difficult to raise, as the cocks will often kill the hens, and the chicks require live insects. A beautiful pheasant, large, with a tremendously long tail, coppery buff and

Reeves' Pheasant *(Syrmaticus reevesi)*

Elliot's Pheasant *(Syrmaticus ellioti)*

chestnut marked with black and white. Bad-tempered and quarrelsome; a cock will do for several hens, but these will fight and must be kept in separate pens.

When a compatible pair can be found, these birds are good breeders and lay abundantly. There are quite a few at present in North America and Europe.

There are three main subspecies: **Scintillating Copper Pheasant** (*S.s. scintillans*) from the northern islands of Japan. The male has a spotted white, black and chestnut body. It is the most widely kept and bred in captivity.

Soemmerring's Copper Pheasant *(S. s. soemmerringi)* from the northern half of the southern island of Kyushu; chestnut and black, darker and more uniform, but also richer in color. They're often kept and reared in captivity.

Ijima's Copper Pheasant (*S.s. ijimae*) from the south of Kyushu, is similar, also dark, with a silvery white patch on the rump. It is the most beautiful of the three; also the rarest.

Another species of Long-tailed Pheasant, **Mrs. Hume's Bar-tail** (*S. humiae*), from northern Burma and neighboring countries, has seldom been kept, and never bred, in captivity until 1965, when some arrived in England. They proved easy to keep and bred freely, and they soon became numerous in pheasantries.

Melanistic mutant

It resembles Elliot's Pheasant but is darker, particularly the head, neck and belly, which are blackish gray.

Mikados and Elliots are often kept and reared, but not too commonly. Reeves' Pheasant has been well established, even as a game bird.

TRUE PHEASANTS

The True Pheasants, or Game Pheasants (genus *Phasianus*), have an extensive range in the wild state, from the Caucasus to Japan. They have adapted themselves to new climates and become naturalized in many parts of the world. A number of females can be kept with one cock. There are many kinds, all more or less similar, the Japanese Greens being the most peculiar and handsome. The best known in captivity and coverts are the Blackneck, the Mongolian, the Chinese Ringneck, the Formosan and the Melanistic Mutant. Eggs of game pheasants are small, uniform olive brown, eight to fifteen; incubation usually 24-25 days.

Black-necked Pheasant (*P. colchicus*). From the Caucasus; large, uniform coppery red, with dark green head and neck;

shoulders brown. Hens rather dark and strongly mottled. It was the first pheasant introduced into western Europe.

The so-called English Ringneck is similar, but shows a white collar. It is just a hybrid between the Black-necked and Mongolian or Chinese Ringneck, not a pure or stable race.

Mongolian Pheasant (*P. mongolicus*). A very large bird, with a violet neck and broad white collar, white shoulders and general plumage dark red glossed with green. Female pale and little marked below. Game bird from Central Asia.

Chinese Ringneck Pheasant (*P. torquatus*). Rather small, but brightly colored; a broad white collar, dark red breast, yellow upper-back, gray shoulders, orange flanks and green rump. Female, rather pale. Found in most parts of China, except western China. A very good game bird, widely introduced in America.

Formosan Pheasant (*P. formosanus*). Similar to the Chinese Ringneck, but paler, with a broad white neck ring. Female, very

Formosan Pheasant *(Phasianus formosanus)* and female

Golden Pheasant *(Chrysolophus pictus)*

pale. The stock in America often is too pale and partly albinistic, not normally colored.

Melanistic Mutants originated within feral stock in Europe one hundred years ago. At first, cocks were darker all over than Black-necks with a great deal of blue and green on the breast; the female was mahogany brown. Gradually, the cocks have become entirely dark glossy green and blue and the female greenish black. They are fine birds, strong and vigorous, evidently better suited to the coverts of Europe than the Asiatic forms. Very ornamental.

Green Pheasant (*Phasianus versicolor*) resembles the other game pheasants but is solid green on the neck and underparts. A very good game bird, native to Japan, and a distinct species.

GOLDEN PHEASANT, AMHERST'S PHEASANT

The Golden and Amherst's Pheasants (genus *Chrysolophus*) are highly suitable for aviaries. They are small, incredibly beautiful, hardy, tame, easy to keep and to raise. They come from central and western China and have been thoroughly acclimatized. All beginners should start with one or both of these marvelous species. Several hens can be kept with one cock. Breed normally the second year, but often the first in captivity.

Swinhoe's Pheasant *(Lophura swinhoei)*

Golden Pheasant *(Chysolophus pictus)*

Golden Pheasant (*C. pictus*). A lovely small bird from central China. The cock has a large yellow crest, orange ruff, barred with black, green mantle, maroon shoulders, blue wings, yellow back and scarlet underparts; tail brown with red feathers near the base, spotted black. First year cock resembles females, but larger, with yellow and red tinges and larger ruff. Long reared in captivity and very suitable for small pens. Eggs creamy white; incubation 23 days.

Dark-throated Golden Pheasant. A mutation of the Golden, produced in captivity about 100 years ago. The cock is generally darker and has blackish face and throat; the tail barred instead of spotted. The female is chocolate brown. Chicks are blackish brown with white spots. This mutation breeds true.

Professor A. Ghigi, Bologna, Italy, recently has fixed a yellow mutation which breeds true. The cock is yellow all over, except for black borders to the orange feathers of the ruff, and the blue patch on the wings. The female is pale buff with gray markings. A very interesting and pretty bird. A darker "Salmon" mutation has since been established, and a "Cinnamon" one has lately become well established in America.

Amherst's Pheasant (*C. amherstiae*). Replaces the Golden in western China. Just as easy to keep and hardy. The magnificent cock has a dark green head with a small scarlet crest; ruff white and black; mantle green; wings blue; back yellow; rump red; tail white barred with black, very long and soft, and orange-tipped feathers at the base; breast green; belly white. Bill and legs gray. Pure specimens must have a small red crest, a green crown, no red underneath and a clearly barred tail. Females are reddish brown barred with black, with no yellow tinge; the bill and legs are bluish gray. First year cocks brown, with a short grayish ruff and a whitish tail. Eggs creamy buff, six to twelve; incubation 23 days.

PEACOCK PHEASANTS

The Peacock Pheasants (genus *Polyplectron*) are quite peculiar in aspect and habits. They live in the deep forests of the eastern Himalayas, Burma, Indo-China, Hainan, Malaysia and Palawan. They eat mostly grubs, berries and fallen fruit. In captivity, they must be fed ground meat, insects and fruit. They are small and their plumage is brown, vermiculated with buff; their wings and

Golden Pheasant *(Chrysolophus pictus)*, female.

tail are marked with large spots or splashes of metallic green and blue. Females smaller and duller. There are seven species, all of which have bred in captivity. The Gray, or Chinquis, and the Germain are the best known and have been raised very often; so has the very beautiful Palawan. Grays and Germains are fairly hardy, particularly the Gray, and they require a heated shelter only if the temperature drops below 20 degrees F. They lay clutches of two eggs only, but if these are removed, they may lay five times between March and June. It is best to set eggs as soon as possible, as they do not keep as well as many other pheasant eggs. Also use a lightweight hen, as the eggs and chicks are very small. When possible, use a hen known to be a good "caller," as the young, for the first few days, feed only from the mother's bill and refuse to pick up food from the ground. When you are unfortunate and select a hen that does not call, then place a mealworm on the end of a sharp-pointed stick and hold it just above their heads. The

35

Mikado Pheasant and female (*Syrmaticus mikado)*

Common Koklass *(Pucrasia macrolopha)*

Himalayan Blood Pheasant (*Ithaginis cruentus cruentus*)

worms will wiggle and attract their attention. Usually they will reach for it.

When feeding worms to the young, it is advisable first to feed the hen all the grains she will eat, as then she is more likely to be big-hearted and call the young.

Peacock Pheasants are very light eaters, both young and adult. When the young are 24 hours old, it is time enough to start offering grit and worms. They will eat an average of six worms per day each. After the first week, they will usually start picking up worms, egg, and small pieces of greens. From this time on they can be handled the same as other young pheasants.

Often when you lack sufficient eggs for a full setting, you can make up the difference with Golden Pheasants' eggs—the young do well together. No need to worry—the little Peacock Pheasants

Gray Peacock Pheasant *(Polyplectron bicalcaratum)*.

Congo Peacock
(Afropavo congensis)

will take care of themselves and get their full share of food. Young Peacock Pheasants have a peculiar trait of hiding under the mother's tail and come forward only when called. If the hen happens to be without a tail, they get back where the tail should be. This trait is probably a necessary protection in their native haunts. The sex of Peacock Pheasants is difficult to determine during the first few months. About this time the male will be slightly larger, with a longer tail. When adult, the ocelli are round, darker and more accentuated, while the markings on the female are arrow-shaped. They come into full plumage in their second year. About this time the cocks start to develop spurs, but not always. I note that the cocks without spurs breed as well as those with them. Peacock Pheasants begin to lay in their second year. Occasionally

White Peafowl *(Pavo cristatus alb)*

Satyr Tragopan and female *(Tragopan satyra)*

Blue Eared Pheasant *(Crossoptilon auritum)*

Palawan Peacock Pheasant *(Polyplectron emphanum)*

a hen will lay in her first year. The incubation period is 21 days.

Bronze-tailed Peacock Pheasant (*Polyplectron chalcurum*), from the highlands of Sumatra, has a long, narrow tail which cannot be spread, with large patches of metallic green at the tip of the feathers; rest of plumage brown, finely pencilled with black. Female a bit smaller, with a shorter tail, no spur. Rather resembles the Golden Pheasant in shape and voice. Imported and reared in Europe since 1932. Not showy, but interesting and fairly hardy. An allied but better marked species (*P. inopinatum*) inhabits the mountains of Malaysia; has never been kept in captivity.

Germain's Peacock Pheasant (*Polyplectron germaini*), from the hills of southern Annam, is dark brown with blue-green ocelli on the wings and tail, which is broad and can be spread like a fan; face skin red. Female like the male, but the ocelli smaller and triangular, instead of round. Often bred now in America and in Europe.

Gray Peacock Pheasant (*Polyplectron bicalcaratum*). Finely mottled dark gray and white or buff, with large blue and purple ocelli on wings and tail, which is spread in display. Face skin yellow to pale orange. Female much smaller with blackish ocelli. Found from Sikkim to southern China, central Annam and Hainan; several fairly similar subspecies. Hardy and often raised in captivity; very beautiful.

Malay Peacock Pheasant (*Polyplectron malacense*). Has a pointed metallic blue crest, a small ruff and a shorter tail; reddish brown, with large blue-green ocelli. Female smaller, brown. Inhabits the lowlands of Sumatra and Malay. Delicate in captivity; seldom kept and bred unless kept in warm indoor houses, where it does extremely well.

Bornean Peacock Pheasant (*Polyplectron m. schleiermacheri*); extremely rare, only once imported into America and recently reared in California. Close to the Malay, with a shorter crest and a larger metallic ruff.

Palawan Peacock Pheasant (*Polyplectron emphanum*) is a near ally of the Malay; the most beautiful of the genus. The cock has a long black crest, white bands on the face, which is red, the whole mantle and wing coverts metallic green and purple; large ocelli on the tail; underparts black. Female dark brown with a

Golden Pheasant *(Chysolophus pictus)*

Blue Peafowl *(Pavo cristatus)*

white face and throat. Not uncommon in captivity since 1929, and fairly often reared. Needs a shelter in cold districts.

ARGUS PHEASANTS

The Argus Pheasants, (genera *Rheinartia* and *Argusianus*) are related to the Peacock Pheasants, but they are much larger, with tremendous tails. Their plumage shows an amazingly beautiful and complicated pattern of chestnut, brown, white, gray and black spots, ocelli and bars.

Crested Argus have normally shaped wings, but an enormous tail. Great Argus have narrower tails, but huge ornamental wings. All are inhabitants of the forests of Indo-China, Malaya, Sumatra and Borneo, feeding like the Peacock Pheasants on fruit and grubs. Crested Argus are fairly hardy as they live higher up, but Great Argus cannot stand frost and must be well sheltered. They lay clutches of two eggs and require meat, insects and fruit to do well. They breed readily. Despite the quiet tones of their plumage, they are strikingly handsome; their display is remarkable.

Great Argus Pheasant *(Argusianus argus)*

Crested Argus *(Rheinartia ocellata).*

Crested Argus (*Rheinartia ocellata*) is streaked and spotted white or buff on a rich brown background. It has a thick nuchal crest, a white face, a pink bill and tremendously long and broad tail feathers, beautifully marked with reddish spots and ocelli. Female brown, with broad dark bands on the wings. A most striking bird brought over from the mountains of central Annam in 1923 for the first time. Fairly hardy and easy to breed. A few wild caught birds present in captivity. A closely allied subspecies in the mountains of central Malaya (*R. o. nigrescens*).

Malay Great Argus (*Argusianus argus argus*), from the lowlands of Malaya and Sumatra, is the most often seen and reared in aviaries. The male has huge wing coverts, most beautifully decorated with ocelli and complicated patterns of buff, reddish, gray and black; two very long central tail feathers; face and neck

1. *Ringneck Pheasant*

2. *Mongolian Pheasant*

3. *Versicolor Pheasant*

5. *Siamese Fireback Pheasant*

4. *Reeves's Pheasant*

6. *Cheer Pheasant*

7. *Malayan Fireback Pheasant*

8. *Green Junglefowl*

9. *Mikado Pheasant*

10. *White-crested Kaliji Pheasant*

11. Golden Pheasant

12. Silver Pheasant

13. Swinhoe's Pheasant

14. Amherst Pheasant

15. Palawan Peacock-Pheasant

16. Blue Eared Pheasant

17. Satyr Tragopan

18. Impeyan Pheasant

19. Edward's Pheasant

R.A.Vowles

White Peafowl *(Pavo cristatus alb)*

almost naked and blue; red legs. Female with normally shaped wings and tail; brown below, finely marked and barred above. Not hardy, but strong and easy to rear.

Bornean Great Argus (*Argusianus argus grayi*). Similar, but slightly smaller, grayer above, with white spots, more orange below. Otherwise not different. Seldom imported or reared in captivity.

PEAFOWLS

The Peafowls (*Pavo*) are well known. There are two species: the Indian, or Blue, which is very commonly kept, and the Green, or Spicifer, which comes from Burma, Siam, Indo-China, Malaya and Java. The White and Black-winged are color varieties of the Blue, and the Spalding a cross between the Blue and the Green.

Indian Peafowls are hardy and sociable; they can be kept at liberty almost anywhere, the only drawback being their tiresome and loud voice, and their propensity to eat flowers and vegetables in a small garden. The Green, a much taller, more beautiful bird, with a long, straight crest, is not hardy and has a savage disposition which obliges one to isolate cocks, which often attack people and may prove dangerous to children. They are, therefore, better kept in pens. But they are such fine birds that it is worthwhile building a large cage for them.

While peafowl do not mature until the third year, two-year-old hens lay fertile eggs. Adult hens will lay as many as twenty-three eggs a season, if the eggs are removed and the hens are not allowed to set. When raising peafowl with chickens, use large hens, such as the Rhode Island Red or Plymouth Rock, either of which will take six peafowl eggs, and when all six eggs hatch they can brood the young. The period of incubation is from 28 to 30 days. It is advisable to turn the eggs by hand once a day, as some hens are unable to turn them as they should, perhaps because the nest is too deep. Handle and feed both adults and young according to instructions given for pheasants.

Circular pheasant shelter with separate runs for each different species emanating from central enclosed quarters housing separate sections for each breed

Brown Eared Pheasant *(Crossoptilon mantchurium)*

Gray Peacock Pheasant *(Polyplectron bicalcaratum)*

Green Peafowl *(Pavo muticus)*.

Indian Peafowl (*Pavo cristatus*). A common and well-known bird. The adult male has the neck blue and the wing coverts barred buff and black. Female dark brown above, with green on the neck. It is found wild in India and Ceylon and it has long been domesticated. Two mutations have occurred in captivity, the White and Black-shouldered; the latter with dark blue and green wing-coverts in the male, the female being whitish with buff and gray markings. Pied Peacocks are also found, having irregular patches.

Green Peafowl (*Pavo muticus*). Occurs in Burma (duller and bluer (*P. m. spiciferus*), Siam and Indo-China (*P. m. imperator*), Malaya and Java (*P. m. muticus*).

These magnificent birds are much taller than the Indian Peafowl. They have a straight crest, blue and yellow skin on the face, ocellated green neck and breast. Females like the male, only a little duller, with short green tail. Not very hardy.

CONGO PEACOCK

The **Congo Peacock** *(Afropavo congensis)* is the only African pheasant. It was discovered forty years ago in deep forest. The size of the Rhode Island Red chicken, the male has a short tail, but is crested, dark green with blue wings; the hen is light chestnut and bright coppery green. Seven birds reached the New York Zoo in 1947, but the one hen soon died. A great rarity. Two males have lived in the Bronx Zoo over ten years. A certain number of them reached the Antwerp Zoo later on, and young birds have been reared there and at the Rotterdam Zoo They require planted indoor aviaries to be successful.

Shelter for Pheasants

Pheasants as a whole are unusually hardy and require very little shelter—and that mostly from the sun. The jungle species, especially, dislike sunshine.

For shelter in tropical and sub-tropical regions, a wire-covered run with bushes or shrubbery for shade is good. In cold climates, the birds should be protected from the sun in summer and winds in winter. True, they will live in the open, but it is better to make them comfortable in order to keep mortality low. Cold and snow do not bother them as much as dampness and drafts. Regardless of the type of building you may provide, they will roost inside during the day and outside at night. In any kind of weather, they are better off roosting outside than in a damp, drafty building.

In Maryland, an open-front shed is good for all but the tropical species such as Argus, Firebacks, etc. The shed should have ample head room in the front and should be at least eight feet deep, with openings in the back to allow free circulation of air in the summer. Without these openings, the shed becomes an air pocket and is an extremely hot place during the day. Of course, the rear openings are closed during cold weather. Such a shed provides a roosting place out of the sun, keeps the dust bath dry and protects the feed and drinking water from the sun and rain.

In extremely cold sections, the front can be partially closed with boards and the remainder sheltered by a removable muslin-covered frame. Glass should never be used, because the inside will be very hot while the sun is shining on it and will be just as cold after the sun sets. The muslin permits a free circulation of air and a more even temperature.

If possible, the pheasant pen site should face south and be well drained. Avoid wet ground; a constantly wet pen is injurious to the birds.

Common Koklass *(Pucrasia macrolopha macrolopha)*

Silver Pheasant *(Lophura nycthemera)*

Amherst's Pheasant *(Chrysolophus amherstiae)*

SHELTER FOR TROPICAL PHEASANTS

Experience indicates that tropical pheasants require heat when the temperature falls below 32 degrees F. It is true that some breeders have been able to bring them through sub-zero weather without heat (as I have myself), but this method is not good. Considering the value of the birds, the risk is too great.

Not too many years ago, one could risk wintering the tender species without heat, but why take the chance now when the birds have increased in value? Insulating material can be bought for a relatively modest price, and a first-class oil or coal-burning, hot-water garage heater can be obtained for a modest sum. This type heater uses very little fuel and requires attention only twice daily. In choosing a heating plant, safety should be stressed; the lives of your birds and the value of your plant are worth consideration. It is bad business—it is folly, in fact—to take any chance of loss from freezing when absolute protection can be had for the price of a few pairs. Peace of mind alone is worth more than the cost.

It is very possible that many of the species now considered rare will be extremely difficult, if not impossible, to get in the near future, because they have been driven farther and farther into the jungle; some are already doomed to extinction.

UNHEATED WINTER QUARTERS FOR TENDER SPECIES

Select a dry building with a wooden floor well off the ground. Make the floor double thickness with tar paper between. Place an opening in the south front only and make it just large enough to admit the light. Cover the openings, both inside and out, with a good grade of unbleached muslin. Cover the floor with five inches of peat; on top of this spread eight to twelve inches of loose, dry straw. Well toward the rear, away from the muslin-covered openings, place removable perches made from boards four inches wide by two inches deep with rounded corners. Pheasants like rounded perches, such as the handles of rakes or brooms; however, such perches are unsuitable for cold weather, as they let the toes curl under, and without the protection of the breast feathers, they soon freeze. The wide roosts keep the toes straight out and covered. The feet are the most sensitive part of the pheasant and therefore the first to freeze.

During extremely cold weather remove the roosts, thus compelling the birds to squat in the straw.

HEATED QUARTERS

For several years I have used a modified type of Monitor poultry house for winter quarters for the birds. This building has proved satisfactory in every respect. I have not had a single case of sickness due to drafts, cold or too much heat. The one disadvantage is that the keeper must pass through each pen to feed and water, which may excite the birds and cause them to injure them-

Enlarged detail of circular pheasant shelter showing Dr. D.R. Baylis, Berkshire, England, feeding an eared pheasant.

Cheer Pheasant *(Catreus wallichi)*

Malay Great Argus *(Argusianus argus argus)*

Ceylon Junglefowl (*Gallus lafayettei*)

selves. A passageway could be added to the back by raising the roof, but this would necessitate heating considerably more cubic feet of space and would be of no advantage to the birds. The building is lined throughout with a good grade of insulating material. It is heated by an automatic hot-water garage heater, which has kept a 55 degree F. temperature, for which it was set when installed. The operation of the heater is economical and requires attention only twice a day.

All openings in the building are covered with muslin. The upper openings are kept closed during winter; the lower are open during the day, except in extremely cold weather. The floor is of double thickness with heavy tar paper between, covered with five inches of peat and eight inches of loose straw. The boiler room has a cement floor, and the walls are covered with a fireproof material. (By making the boiler room larger than necessary, space is available to sprout oats in the winter months.) Partitions are of boards two feet high, the remaining space covered with one-inch netting. Because the building is fourteen feet deep, I allow ten feet in width for Argus (140 square feet), and seven feet for Fireback (98 square feet), which I find adequate for the short time they are confined. All openings are two feet square and covered with a good grade of muslin. The upper openings are so placed that they let the sun reach the rear of the building at noon; the lower openings take care of the front. No glass is used, except for a small window in the boiler room.

When only a few pair are kept and the heat is not carried any distance, a coal-burning stove or other inexpensive heater can be used. Other types of buildings can, of course, be adapted to the situation, but the general requirements are constant.

SHELTER FOR GAME PHEASANTS

Most individuals or groups rearing pheasants for later release in the fall, or when full plumage is attained, need make no provision for shelter during the winter months.

If the small pen system, discussed in the chapters on breeding and runs, is being used, a small shelter must be provided for protection from the sun and storms. Should the large pen system be used, several lean-to or cornshock shelters should be provided.

If kept in small quantities during the winter months, protection

Malay Crested Fireback *(Lophura rufa)*

similar to that outlined specifically for the ornamental species may be used. However, since these birds can winter the severe weather of the northern sections of the United States, such careful measures do not have to be taken. Shelter capable of withstanding the weight of snow and ice must be provided.

Although most groups will have set these pheasants at liberty soon after they get full plumage, the responsibility of the agency releasing the birds should not end until provision for winter feeding has been made.

Himalayan Monal, female *(Lophophorus impeyanus)*

Edwards's Pheasant (*Lophura edwardsi*)

Ijima's Copper Pheasant (*Syrmaticus soemmerringi ijimae*)

Swinhoe's Pheasant *(Lophura swinhoei)* in enclosure

Run Construction And Treatment

Although both open and closed runs can be used for pheasants, closed runs are best for all ornamental pheasants and most game pheasants. Only those birds being raised on a large scale as game birds should be kept in open pens. Rare pheasants are too valuable to risk losing. With open runs, the birds must be either wing-clipped or pinioned, thereby rendering them easy prey for their enemies. Besides, a pinioned bird can do as much damage to itself with one full wing as it can with two. However, when pheasants must be kept in open runs, clipping is recommended. Instructions for clipping and brailing will be found in the chapter on rearing.

CLOSED RUN CONSTRUCTION

The outside walls of all pheasant pens should be as vermin-proof as it is possible to make them; the better the construction, the less trouble will be experienced. You may think this slightly more expensive construction is unnecessary, because there are no weasels, mink or skunks in the neighborhood of the pens. However, a single visit from a weasel would cost more than the extra expense of good construction.

In constructing outside walls, I always put eighteen inches of galvanized iron at the top; this is sold as flashing. It is fastened securely to the top runner. Then three feet of half-inch hardware cloth is fastened to the iron with galvanized hog rings; then I put two feet of boards at the bottom. To the bottom board I fasten eighteen inches of half-inch hardware cloth, which is to be buried in the ground; the earth is replaced and packed hard. All knotholes and cracks should be covered with half-inch mesh hardware cloth. This type of construction is slightly more expensive in the beginning than the ordinary poultry netting construction, but it is

White-crested Kalij (*Lophura hamiltoni*)

Opposite:

Black-breasted Kalij
   (*Lophura lathami*)

much cheaper in the end. It will outlast the cheaper construction four or five times. Besides, you will have the satisfaction of knowing that you have done everything possible to protect your birds.

If you can afford to go to even greater lengths, another and even more thorough method of making the pens vermin-proof is to wire over all sides and roof with half-inch mesh, which admits nothing more than an occasional young mouse that can be easily destroyed. This method excludes all dangerous predators, including rats and snakes, and even sparrows and other small wild birds, which may carry vermin and disease. Chain mesh is preferable to hardware cloth, and also looks more attractive and lighter.

The buried wire netting can be replaced by a concrete or brick wall two feet deep, leaving one or two inches exposed above the ground. This will exclude burrowing animals, if the ground around the wall is level and sound. In contrary cases, it may be necessary to make the wall deeper.

Top construction is dependent in part on location and weather. If your locality is not subject to heavy, wet, snow and sleet, the uprights can be spaced farther apart and one-inch poultry netting can be used. In Maryland and many other sections, we are subject to severe winters, and the four-inch by four-inch uprights must not be spaced over eight feet apart each way, and two-inch mesh netting is used, as the smaller the mesh, the more snow and ice it will accumulate. On the two-inch mesh netting, I have often seen snow and ice from two to five inches thick. A few hundred square feet of ice and snow will weigh many hundreds of pounds. For top framing, use two-inch by four-inch boards set up the two-inch way.

Should you make the roof of the pen half-inch netting, it is necessary to have it pitch at a high angle in a snowy district so that the snow runs off and can be easily removed. It must be very strongly supported.

In very wet sections, it is advantageous to have part of the roof solidly covered. It is always advisable, however, to leave part of the roof exposed to rain, which is beneficial to the birds as long as they can be sheltered from it, if they wish.

I usually make inside partitions with boards two feet high at the bottom; two-inch poultry mesh netting will do for the remainder. Be careful to have the bottom board flush with the ground to keep birds from getting under them and into the next pen. The two-foot boards are necessary to keep the cocks from fighting.

It is not always necessary to place two-foot boards around the pens if you do not place birds of the same, or closely related, species next to one another. The pens look better without them. But in such a case, small mesh wire netting should replace the boards, so that the birds cannot get their heads through the partition.

More elaborate and durable pens can be built of steel frames. It is important that they be vermin-proof.

All gates should fit tightly, open out, and be of a width that will admit a wheelbarrow or fair-size crate. They must fasten securely with a hasp and be hung on heavy brass hinges, to insure their being closed at all times.

Many breeders prefer to divide each run into two compartments by a partition in the middle. One of the compartments should have a wire door which can be closed or opened. This permits the cock to be separated from the hen in case of fights, egg-eating, illness, etc., without catching the birds, which is always dangerous.

For the smaller species, such as Golden and Amherst, pens allowing twelve feet by six feet per bird are sufficient. For the larger birds, nine feet by eighteen feet is recommended. Of course, the larger the better.

RUNS FOR GAME PHEASANTS

Individuals raising the game pheasants, as a hobby or for commercial purposes on a small scale, will find the preceding sections, dealing primarily with run construction for the ornamental species, of interest. The methods outlined are well proven but too expensive for a propagation program. The runs discussed here are for use with brooders and breeding pens.

Shelter pens are required in conjunction with both types of brooder houses discussed in the chapter on rearing. In the event that the small double house is used, two shelter pens, twelve by twelve by six feet high, are required; and for the larger brooder house, a large shelter pen, twelve by twenty-four by six feet high, is necessary. The shelter pens are boarded at least two feet from the ground to protect young birds from driving rains and drafts. The sides of the pen must be wired with a one-inch mesh, pre-

Elliot's Pheasant *(Syrmaticus ellioti)*

Southern Green Pheasant *(Phasianus versicolor versicolor)*

Edwards's Pheasant, female (*Lophura edwardsi*)

ferably 19 gauge netting. It is advisable to cover the top of the pen with a two-inch mesh before the addition of the top covering, which may consist of boards, canvas or hay, because the shelter pen must shed water.

The shelter pen is very important; it is used as a shelter when the birds no longer use the house and also serves as adequate protection in case of storms.

The most essential parts of the entire brooder system are large runs. Because of the cost involved in building the proper sized runs, many persons try to skimp on the size only to find out that the value involved in losses resulting from cannibalism and from overcrowding far exceed the original cost of the necessary equipment.

If the small double house is used, two runs are required. Each should measure approximately thirty-six feet wide by ninety-six feet long. These runs should be covered on the top. One should construct the side fence of one-inch mesh wire and the top covering of two-inch mesh wire. In building the runs, it is more practical to make them long and narrow, rather than square, because it is much simpler to cover the runs with wire, and easier to drive the birds, should a storm make it necessary to hurry them.

If the large house is used, the large run is not partitioned. It should measure approximately seventy-five feet wide by ninety-six feet long. The wire netting of the side fence should be of one-inch mesh, while the top covering can be of two-inch mesh. The size and position of supports must be determined by the locale and circumstances involved.

Many types of brooder houses and pens are satisfactory. However, the types of equipment suggested above have been thoroughly proven. The pen dimensions given provide the required twenty-four square feet per chick, and standard 150 foot rolls of six-foot netting can be used satisfactorily without waste, when the runs are covered.

TREATMENT OF RUNS

Pheasant runs must be kept clean if you wish to have healthy birds; filth and health do not go together. Cleanliness and proper food are the two most important requisites for healthy birds. When you keep pheasants, you may expect visitors. So, be

Tragopan in outdoor run planted with grass

Scintillating Copper Pheasant *(Syrmaticus soemmerringi scintillans)*

Reeves' Pheasant *(Syrmaticus reevesi)*

Elliot's Pheasant *(Syrmaticus ellioti)*

Ceylon Junglefowl (*Gallus lafayettei*)

prepared. See that visitors are impressed by your neatness and cleanliness.

Loose feathers and droppings should be swept up frequently; droppings will accumulate mostly under the roosts. The ground under the roosts should be broken and mixed with sand. When cleaning, remove this loose earth and replace it with clean, fresh sand.

Once a year, preferably in the fall, the run should be covered with chloride of lime or sprinkled with a strong salt solution. I prefer the salt because it is odorless, clean, easy to apply and very effective. This salt solution is made of a coarse, cheap salt (rock salt). Into a barrel filled with water, place a quantity of salt wrap-

White Eared Pheasants *(Crossoptilon crossoptilon)* in indoor shelter

ped in cheese cloth, and plunge it up and down until the water will float an egg. Apply with a sprinkling can after a heavy rain, while the ground is still soft, as it will penetrate deeper than when the ground is dry. Furthermore, the worms come up to feed and are nearer the surface after a rain. It is surprising how many worms the salt will kill; this is the object of the salt solution, because the worms carry the cyst of the gape and other worms injurious to pheasants and poultry. Of course, the birds must be removed before the salt is applied.

It is best to plant pens with shrubs and grasses, which provide useful shelter and create a congenial environment conducive to breeding. Care must be taken not to use disinfectants harmful to vegetation. Poisonous and too rapidly growing plants must be avoided. The thick, bushy types are often preferable, but others also may be useful by providing perches. Suitable species are numerous and should be selected according to climate. Lawns and grasses grown in the pens are good and an excellent source of fresh green food. Rape, alfalfa and clover make excellent cover crops and for the shelter pen and large run. Rape is perhaps the most practical, because it has a sturdier stem, grows fast and is not easily killed out by the birds. Rape can be broadcast about twelve pounds to the acre.

Should you be raising day-old chicks gotten from a state agency, planting the rape between April 15 and May 1 should give adequate time for the cover crop to take hold before the chicks arrive, although special climate considerations may have to be made.

If the cover crop becomes too heavy, strips should be mowed throughout the pen to give the ground a chance to sweeten and enable the birds to move about more readily.

If no cover crop in the shelter pen or run is provided, fresh green food in the form of lawn clippings or chopped lettuce should be given. Green food must never be piled up, though, because it will ferment.

Domestic fowl *(Gallus gallus)*

Siamese Fireback *(Lophura diardi)*

Satyr Tragopan *(Tragopan satyra)*

Impeyan Monal *(Lophophorus impeyanus)* and female

Breeding Pheasants

Only the best should be considered when selecting breeding stock. Never look for so-called "bargains," because they seldom turn out to be good breeders. Remember that although the preponderance of breeders are reputable business people, dishonesty can more readily occur in this industry than in many others. Birds are not always what they appear to be on the surface. For instance, a bird can be in perfect plumage and yet be in an advanced stage of tuberculosis; a hen can have ovaritis so severely that she will never lay a fertile egg, even though she is in perfect plumage and flesh.

Contact some reputable breeder of long experience when selecting breeding pheasants. He should be one who has been in the business long enough to know how to select the best birds and crate them so that they will arrive in good condition. In other words, one whose interest does not end with the sale. Few, if any, experienced breeders have any idea of profit. They breed only for the love of these exotic birds, and they desire others to share the pleasure they find. Moreover, if you experience trouble, a reliable breeder will gladly supply wholesome advice—freely and fully. The slight difference in the original cost will be offset many times by the permanent satisfaction you have in knowing that you have the best that can be had.

Hatching eggs appeals to some as an economical way of starting a pheasant collection, although I have found it to the contrary. Among my pheasant-breeding friends, there is not one who wants to sell eggs of rarer species. When inveigled into selling, it is only at the buyer's risk, and no guarantee of fertility is made. It is also well to know that eggs can be "doctored" to prevent hatching, and that often this "doctoring" cannot be detected by experts. For example, the eggs of the Araucana Fowl, a rumpless chicken from

Mikado Pheasant (*Syrmaticus mikado*)

Malay Crested Fireback (*Lophura rufa*)

Himalayan Blood Pheasant, female *(Ithaginis cruentus cruentus)*

Cheer Pheasant *(Catreus wallichi)*

Chile, are the same pale blue color and the same size and shape as the eggs of the Brown Eared Pheasants. Turkey eggs are similar to those of the Himalayan Impeyan Pheasant.

Pheasants should be bought in the early fall for breeding the following season. At that time breeders have the season's crops on hand and prices are low, but the prices become higher later in the season. Birds placed in strange quarters in the early fall become accustomed to their new home and are more likely to breed than birds shipped and placed in strange pens just before the breeding season.

PACKING AND SHIPPING

Pheasants should always be dispatched in closed baskets or cases, the tops of which are made of cloth or canvas padded with straw or other soft material. This will avoid damage to the head. For short trips of less than three days, no drinking water is needed, if greens and soaked bread have been supplied. Enough air will be gotten if a few small holes are made. Air transportation is quickest and best. For long sea travel, cases with wooden barred fronts and movable troughs are necessary; there should be a flap in front of the bars and a well-padded top.

MATING

Breeding birds that have proved satisfactory are left as they are, so long as they continue to give strong, fertile eggs. New matings are made in the fall, as soon as it is possible to select the strongest and best-developed birds, and they are placed together at once in their new pens. This gives them ample time to become accustomed to each other and to their new quarters. This method has proved far superior to mating just before the breeding season, and it has greatly reduced the loss of females due to killing by the cock. However, if compelled to mate at breeding time, place the cock with the hen in her quarters. If this is not possible, place both in a strange pen.

Because many pheasant cocks are extremely pugnacious, it is not advisable to have more than one in the same pen with a hen. It is not always safe to keep two or more together without hens, in or out of the breeding season; they are likely to fight at any time, and

Silver Pheasant *(Lophura nycthemera),* female

Sonnerat's Junglefowl *(Gallus sonnerati)*

White Eared Pheasant (*Crossoptilon crossoptilon crossoptilon*)

a fight usually results in the death of one or both. Quite frequently two hens in a pen with a cock will fight. When this happens, it is best to separate them, as in the majority of cases only the eggs of one hen will be fertile. If you must use one cock for two females, separate the hens and alternate the male every other day. Some males will mate with more than one hen. My best success has been with one hen to a cock with the following genera and species: Impeyan, Tragopans, Argus, Firebacks, Berlioz and Silver. In the case of others I have mated as many as five hens to one male with fair results. However, three hens to one male will give a higher incidence of fertility.

During the breeding season, shelter must be placed in the pens for the protection of the hens; in fact, it is advisable to provide shelter at all times. Bushes, evergreen boughs or cornstalks may be used. Often the hens will make a nest and lay under this cover. This saves many eggs, as the hens are likely to lay anywhere, not to mention the roost. It is best to have loose straw under the roosts during the breeding season. Also have open-top nest boxes high above the ground. Tragopans, Argus and Peacock pheasants like these elevated nest boxes. Frequently the Mikados and Silvers use them, thus saving many eggs from being broken or eaten.

PINIONING AND BRAILING

Opinion varies as to the advisability of pinioning ornamental pheasants. The advantage is that pinioned birds cannot fly up violently and smash their skulls on the roof of the pens, as they are inclined to do when frightened. It has the drawback of making them clumsy, and it may cause accidents when they fly down from their perches. Also, pinioned hens have more difficulty in escaping attacking cocks. It is often advantageous to pinion the cock and leave the female full-winged, when bad-tempered species are concerned.

Pinioning is a permanent operation. It consists of sectioning the tip of the wing, which represents the hand, close to the small protuberance representing the thumb, which should remain. All the flight feathers are inserted on the hand and are therefore removed forever. It is best to tie the wing with a thin, strong string just before the operation, which is effected with scissors or a snipper. The instruments should be blunted so that the cut is not too sharp. Iodine, ferrous chlorine or another antiseptic is applied to

The small pen system of breeding at the Wisconsin State Experimental Game and Fur Farm

the wound. Unless infection sets in, pinioning is a minor operation and the bird feels little discomfort. The younger the bird, the easier the operation.

When only temporary inability to fly is required, the simplest method is to cut short the flight feathers, or primaries; the first eight or ten feathers of the wing, starting from the tip. No other feathers should be cut. The feathers will grow again when the pheasant next molts.

Brailing means tying the primaries to the secondaries, so as to prevent extension of the wing, and therefore, flight. It can be useful, but it may untie, and the discomfort to the bird is greater than in pinioning. A more detailed description of the methods of clipping and brailing is in the chapter on rearing pheasants.

THE SMALL PEN SYSTEM OF BREEDING

The small pen or harem of breeding pheasants is used on many game farms in the United States. Five or six hens and one cock are placed in a movable pen, twelve feet square and six feet high. The pen may be covered with a two-inch mesh netting. The pen should be boarded about two feet from the bottom.

To avoid unnecessary disturbance of the pheasants while feeding, it is desirable to feed and water from outside the pen. A

Cheer Pheasant *(Catreus wallichi)*

Cheer Pheasant, female *(Catreus wallichi)* on nest

hopper with two sections—one for mash and grain and another for grit, charcoal, and oyster shells—is placed on the outside and a horizontal slot cut in the board base to enable the birds to reach for food.

Pheasants require a laying mash with a high protein content. Most commercial turkey laying mashes may be fed with good results.

A water pan is placed next to the feeding hopper. A vertical slot is used in connection with the water pan, because a horizontal slot prevents the birds from raising their heads when drinking. It is very important that a fresh supply of water be kept before the birds at all times.

To provide shelter from the sun and storms, a small shelter two feet wide by three feet long should be built in one corner of the pen.

In many cases the pheasant hens will lay their eggs under these shelters, and it is advisable to hinge them to one side of the pen so that they may be lifted to enable one to remove the eggs with minimum difficulty. If breeding pens are used to keep birds during the winter, additional brush or cornstalk shelters should be provided.

Breeding pheasants should be placed in breeding pens by March 1. The pens should be moved to fresh ground at least three times during the breeding season. This will help to maintain the health of the pheasants and provide a fresh supply of green food; green food should be available at all times during the mating season.

THE LARGE PEN SYSTEM OF BREEDING

The large pen system is used a lot in large farm operations and propagation programs. Under this plan it is customary to place 100 hens and fifteen to twenty cocks in a pen, allowing at least 100 square feet per bird. Such pens are enclosed by a seven- or eight-foot fence having a two-foot strand of three-fourths inch mesh wire on the lower part and a two-inch mesh on the upper portion of the fence. The small mesh wire should be buried at least six to twelve inches in the ground, the earth replaced and packed hard.

The equipment cost in the large pen system is perhaps less, but the results are not usually as satisfactory as the small pen system. In the large pen system the egg production is a much different procedure. Ordinary commercial feeding hoppers and waterers

Mongolian pheasants at ages (from left): two days, eight days, five weeks, seven weeks, and one year. Below is shown a fully plumed adult Mongolian pheasant

Temminck's Tragopan *(Tragopan temmincki)*

Domesticated Red Cock *(Gallus gallus)*

Malay Peacock Pheasant *(Polyplectron malacense)*

may be placed throughout the pen. The food mixtures remain the same.

If ordinary watering pans are used, a covering should be built over them in order to prevent contamination. A plentiful supply of fresh water should be kept in front of the birds at all times.

Lean-to cornstalk shelters should be erected in the large breeding pen to provide shade and protection from storms.

While pheasant hens lay a few eggs during the month of April, heavy production cannot be expected until the middle of May. Pheasant hens will usually average from 30 to 40 eggs during the laying period. Early and mid-season eggs have the highest fertility and produce the strongest chicks.

Great care must be taken not to disturb pheasants any more than is absolutely necessary when gathering eggs. To avoid startling the birds, many game breeders whistle while working around the pens. Be careful to avoid any sudden movements.

Eggs should be collected once a day during the early part of the season and twice daily during hot weather. After eggs are collected they should be placed point or small end down in a shallow pan or tray that contains sand or grain. The temperature in the room should be from 50 to 60 degrees. A cellar is an excellent place to store eggs. The eggs should be turned daily to keep the germ alive; however, the point or small end should always be kept down and the egg only tilted in one direction one day and the opposite the next.

The Feeding of Pheasants

Correct food, in proper and suitable amounts, together with regular feeding, is an all-important factor in keeping pheasants in good condition. *It is impossible to overstress the importance of food and cleanliness.* With the correct food and proper care, pheasants will live and produce fertile eggs over a period of eight to twelve years.

In the wild state, pheasants must work for a living; all day long they hunt, scratch and pick, thus getting plenty of exercise. At the same time, they are constantly on the lookout for enemies. In captivity they have nothing to do, except eat. They stand around and get little or no exercise. Pheasants are light feeders, so care must be taken not to overfeed. I have never heard of a pheasant starving to death but have known many that died of overfeeding.

Although widely different rations are used by different breeders, there are certain fundamentals which must be recognized to procure the best results. One of the primary requisites of satisfactory feeding is regularity, both as to the feeding of growing young and the breeding stock. The quantity of food required can be determined only by carefully watching the birds. Of considerable importance also is the difference in ration requirements for the various classes of birds.

RATIONS FOR YOUNG PHEASANTS

Breeders have diverse opinions as to the rations to be used in feeding the young. But here again there are certain fundamental rules which must be observed in order to get the best results. It is the aim in feeding poults to obtain the maximum of growth with the minimum of mortality. Just prior to hatching, a certain quantity of food substance is absorbed. Therefore, the poults do not require feeding until they are twenty-four to forty-eight hours old.

For the first three weeks, the poults should be fed four times

Scintillating Copper Pheasant *(Syrmaticus soemmerringi scintillans)*

White Eared Pheasant *(Crossoptilon crossoptilon crossoptilon)*

Mikado Pheasant and female (left) *(Syrmaticus mikado)*

Interior of small double brooder house in readiness for chicks. Feeders and fountains are positioned to allow a free run to and from the box-type brooder

daily; for the next three weeks, three times daily; after that, twice daily. And they must be fed *regularly*.

Food for the young pheasants should be placed on a board or in a shallow dish; the dish must be frequently scalded and kept perfectly clean. Feed only what the birds will eat in fifteen minutes, removing what is left. If the food that is left is not removed, you invite bowel trouble, and this is difficult to overcome. Fresh clean water and fine grit should be kept before the birds at all times.

The first food may consist of boiled fresh eggs or custard made of one egg to a tablespoonful of milk, baked dry. The first day, use either the boiled egg or custard; after that mix the boiled egg, fresh raw egg or custard with a good grade of commercial growing mash, thoroughly scalded. When using scalded food, allow sufficient time for it to cool and absorb the flavor of the different ingredients; it should be moist, but not wet or sloppy, nor should it be allowed to become sour and ferment. Gradually reduce the ration of egg or custard until at the end of the second week the birds have mash only. Continue with the mash, either moist or dry, gradually adding small grains, such as chick grain, millet or canary seed. The wet mash can be mixed with either water or milk of any kind. When using curd, see that it is free from alum, as this drug interferes with digestion. At all times, the young must have finely cut, juicy greens, such as lettuce, clover, alfalfa or chickweed; give all they will eat. As the poults mature, use larger grain until they are on the regular adult ration.

When poults are not growing properly, increase the volume of milk either in the form of fresh milk to drink or curd fed in a small dish. If maturing too rapidly, reduce mash and increase grain, thus reducing the amount of protein.

MASH ANALYSIS

	Percent
Crude protein, not less than	24.0
Crude fat, not less than	4.5
Crude fiber, not more than	6.5
Carbohydrates	} 40.0
Nitrogen-free extract, not less than	

MASH INGREDIENTS

Wheat standard middlings, yellow corn meal, ground barley, fish meal, meat and bone scraps, dried buttermilk, dried skimmed milk, ground oat groats, wheat and bran, one percent salt, cod-liver-oil extract.

ANALYSIS OF CHICK GRAIN

	Percent
Crude protein, not less than	10.0
Crude fat, not less than	2.0
Crude fiber, not more than	4.0
Carbohydrates	} 55.0
Nitrogen-free extract, not less than	

Himalayan Monal *(Lophophorus impeyanus)*

Elliot's Pheasant *(Syrmaticus ellioti)*

Green Junglefowl (*Gallus varius*)

INGREDIENTS

Cracked yellow corn, wheat, oat, groats, kaffir and milo.

Many breeders at present successfully use only prepared food from the beginning. Those breeders desiring to use the prepared mashes (which are better than those available when Denley wrote the first edition of this book) may use the following plan.

Recent experiments indicate that starting and growing mashes having a high protein content are satisfactory. Most commercial turkey starting and growing mashes are adequate. However, in the

Brown Eared chicks are extremely friendly. Here, they show no fear of taking food from keeper's hand

case of a starting feed, a starting mash in a small kernel form is the most desirable and is a type of food that pheasant chicks will be inclined to start eating immediately.

Starting mash can be fed to pheasants up to the time they are from three to four weeks of age. From that time on, they may be fed a growing mash. Starting and growing mashes usually contain the same ingredients, but the growing mash is in a larger kernel form to prevent waste.

After young pheasants are approximately six weeks of age, a small amount of grain may be added to the feed. This is increased gradually until the ration consists of approximately one-fourth grain and three-fourths mash, up to the end of the tenth week.

Green food should be supplied at all times. Lawn clippings and chopped lettuce can and should be supplied to young pheasants during the first week and thereafter until they can actually secure a plentiful supply of the green food which should be present in the shelter pen and large run.

Fresh water should be kept in front of the birds at all times. Water given to the chicks for the first time should have the chill removed, as cold water will kill day-old chicks. Stones and pebbles should be placed in the trough to keep the chicks from waddling in the water. Any commercial disinfectants used according to directions will be satisfactory. However, special care should be taken to follow the directions carefully when disinfecting drinking water, because too much might injure the chicks.

Some difficult species can be reared only when some live food, such as ant-cocoons and mealworms, are offered to them during the first week or longer.

FOOD FOR ADULTS

In feeding adult birds, a commercial laying mash containing 25 percent animal protein should be before them in hoppers at all times.

Grain and greens are fed twice daily—in the early morning and in the evening. If fed in large quantities once a day, the birds are likely to overtax their digestive systems.

As a basis for a ration which has provided most satisfactory results for a number of years, varied from time to time because of the cost of the different grains, the following is offered:

Germain's Peacock Pheasant *(Polyplectron germaini)*

Reeve's Pheasant *(Syrmaticus reevesi)*

Siamese Fireback (*Lophura diardi*)

	Parts
Kaffir corn (Durra)	2
Wheat	3
Hulled oats	2
Sunflower seed	1
Sprouted oats	5

To this is added, in suitable form, all the green food that the birds will eat the year around. During the summer, cabbage, lettuce, kale, spinach, onions (green—both tops and bulb are used), alfalfa, clover, cantaloupe, watermelon, squash, cucumber and fruits of all kinds can be supplied. During the winter months, use ground alfalfa, alfalfa hay, onions and potatoes boiled with the skins on. All greens are cut fine with a vegetable cutter. Grass is best fed on the sod.

WATER

Clean, cold water is everywhere, except in the pheasant pens. Keepers are prone to overlook this and consider that anything, so long as it is wet, is good enough for pheasants to drink. But this is wrong. *Cleanliness is absolutely essential in keeping birds healthy. Stagnant water and unclean fountains are the most successful disease-breeding means that can be found.*

Select drinking fountains made of one piece of metal; avoid sharp angles that cannot be reached with the end of the finger. Place the fountain in the shade a few inches above the ground. Below the fountain dig a hole twelve inches deep, filling it with coarse gravel. This will allow the water spilled to drain away from the surface, so there won't be a constantly wet area for the breeding of diseases. Each morning, empty the water that is left in the fountain, then dampen a small handful of earth and work it around with the hand to remove the green scum (algae) that forms on the sides. This daily scouring will keep the fountain clean and bright. As an additional measure, it is advisable during the summer to boil the fountain once a month.

SPROUTED OATS

Succulent feed is essential to breeding stock and may be furnished in the form of sprouted oats. I am firmly convinced from my experience that they contain some element which stimulates

110

breeding activity and increases fertility. When using the best grade of seed oats, 80 to 90 percent of the seeds will sprout, yielding about three pounds of sprouts to one pound of seeds; heavy feed oats will sprout less than 60 to 70 percent, and frequently cheap light oats will sprout less than 50 percent. The oats are fed when the sprouts are one and one-half inches long, before they become woody and yellow. When soaking oats for sprouting, fresh water must be used for each lot. If the same water is used repeatedly, it becomes strong, has an offensive odor and contains bacteria that are injurious to the birds; the cylinders must be scalded after each use.

MEALWORMS

Mealworms are the larvae of *Tenebrio molitor,* a beetle that loves the dark. The "worms" are found in bran, meal, flour, in the grain bins, under the grain sacks and in the feed house. Each mealworm, which is yellow in color and about one and one-fourth inches long when full grown eventually (after it has gone through the pupa stage) produces a black beetle about one-half inch long. The eggs are white and covered with a sticky secretion which causes the bran to stick to them. In about two weeks, the eggs hatch into slender white larvae. The larvae reach maturity in about 90 days, continue feeding until cold weather, and then hibernate as larvae, passing into the pupa stage the following spring and remaining in that stage for about two weeks. Mealworms are very valuable food for both young and adult pheasants, being extremely rich in vitamins, particularly A and B.

A simple method of producing mealworms is to secure a number of tin cans having a capacity of about a half-bushel of bran. In the tightly fitting tops, punch a dozen or so small holes; fill the can three-quarters full of bran, place a small handful of worms in each can and cover the bran with a piece of old woolen cloth or blanket slightly dampened (if too wet, it will cause the bran to mold). When a large number of worms are required, it is best to build a galvanized iron-lined bin. All covers must fit tightly to prevent the escape of worms and beetles, as well as to keep out mice and rats. When the beetles appear, pieces of carrots, beets, lettuce, cactus pads or damp bread are placed into the can for them to feed on.

Near the end of the season, a substance resembling fine sand ap-

Hume's Bar-tailed Pheasant (*Syrmaticus humiae humiae*)

Palawan Peacock Pheasant *(Polyplectron emphanum)*

Imperial Pheasant *(Lophura imperialis)*

pears in the bottoms of the cans. This is excrement and shells from the worms and must be removed and replaced with fresh bran. To remove, use a sieve made of mosquito netting; discard only what passes-through.

Mealworms can be purchased at pet or bird stores, where they are sold as food for fish and soft-billed birds.

MAGGOTS

Maggots are an excellent food for young pheasants when properly handled. However, they must be thoroughly cleaned and scalded and fed with discrimination; if not, they are rank poison. Breeding maggots is a very unpleasant task, and the only advantage they have over mealworms is the fact that they can be procured in a few days.

Hang a piece of meat—a pluck will do—where the flies can get to it; in a short time you will find tiny maggots which grow rapidly. Under the meat, place a tub containing half a bushel or more of bran. As the maggots mature, they will drop off into the bran. Remove them from the first tub into another containing fresh bran; leave them there for two or three days. During this time the constant movement through the bran is said to "scour" or remove the extraneous matter—rotten meat. Before they are ready to be used as food, they must be thoroughly scalded with boiling water or baked in an oven and allowed to cool.

Brooding Pheasants

The geographical location of the pheasantry is an important factor in determining the time pheasants start to lay. In Maryland they begin about the middle of March and continue laying until June, regardless of the weather. I once had an Argus who laid on Jan. 16, but late March or early April is usually the time they start. However, I have many times dug Swinhoe's and Elliot's eggs out of the ice and snow and raised young from them.

Eggs should be gathered twice a day, in the early morning and in the evening. When some rare species shows signs of laying, it is well to look in the pen several times a day, thus taking as few chances as possible of losing valuable eggs. Most hens will lay under cover, which is a common vice among pheasants and one that is difficult to overcome. Without success, I have tried almost everything to stop egg eating. I have fed different diets and blown eggs, filled with red pepper or mustard—all to no effect. The best results were obtained by having hard-boiled eggs lying about the run, which the pheasants would eat, until they had eaten so many that they became thoroughly sick of the sight of them. The only sure way of saving eggs is to be on guard when the hen is laying and beat the egg-eater to it.

CARE OF HATCHING EGGS

Eggs for hatching should be placed in a tray filled with grain or sand and kept in a cool, well-ventilated semi-dark place. Never use damp or dusty material to hold the eggs, because the dust fills the pores of the shell. Place eggs with the small end down and turn them once daily, always keeping the small end down. By placing them in the same position, it is easy to see which ones have been turned and which have not.

If you are getting eggs shipped from a state agency or breeder, it is important that you get the setting hens several days before the eggs are expected. However, do not get them until you have been

Ringnecked Pheasant (*Phasianus colchicus torquatus*)

Golden Pheasant *(Chrysolophus pictus)*

notified of the date of arrival, because hens will break up if they are held too long before a setting of eggs is given to them.

Eggs may be held for a few days, but it is advisable to set them as soon as possible. Upon receipt, unpack the eggs and place them point, or small end, down in a shallow tray or pan containing sand or grain. They should be allowed to settle for at least twenty-four hours before being given to the hen. Store them in a cellar or room where a temperature of from 50 to 60 degrees is maintained.

TIME LIMIT OF HATCHING EGGS

Try to set the eggs before they are ten days old; the fresher they are, the better the results. Try to keep together all the eggs of the same size and species. Never place large and small eggs in the same nest, and don't place eggs that require twenty-three days to hatch with those that need twenty-eight days, as the latter will not hatch before the hen wants to leave the nest. (A table of hatching times required for the eggs of most feasible species and genera will be found in Appendix II.)

THE FOSTER MOTHER OR BROODY HEN

A year in advance is none too soon to start thinking of your broody hens to make sure they are free from parasites. If a hen is to raise healthy pheasants, she must be healthy herself. If she is infested with worms, lice or scabies, the young pheasants are almost certain to contract them. It is far better to start with a clean, healthy hen than to doctor young birds later on.

A decided change comes over "biddy" when she wants to "sit." Her timidity usually disappears, and she may develop a war-like disposition, which shows itself when attempts are made to disturb her. The broody hen has been charged with many perversities, i.e., lack of persistence in setting, deserting the nest and causing the eggs to become chilled, breaking eggs and smearing the others, as well as herself, with the contents, trampling the newly-hatched birds, neglecting to hover the birds properly, and even killing them. Indeed, the setting hen does sometimes seem to be possessed of a hellish disposition, which leads to the destruction of the fond hopes of the aviculturist and to his dire disgust when he sees valuable eggs or birds sacrificed. At the same time it may be remembered that most hens are rightly disposed and will do their duty well, if given a fair chance. The fault usually is with the keeper or the conditions he provides.

It is often true that the hen will desert her nest only when forced by attacks of lice, mice and ants. There are also times when she sticks to her task, forfeiting her life as the penalty of the keeper's ignorance or negligence. Under clean and comfortable conditions, gently handled and managed, the setters usually will prevent or overcome the difficulties and disturbances which are likely to at-

Ringneck Pheasant chicks, recently hatched and ready to leave the nest.

tend natural incubation. There is a difference in setting hens, and only experience will determine their individual qualities.

The hens to avoid are those which are too heavy or awkward to manage their own feet, those which are too nervous or "flighty" to admit being handled and those having low body temperatures. On the other hand, a hen that has proved herself a good foster mother—a quality improving with age—should be prized and her

Temminck's Tragopan *(Tragopan temmincki)*

Indian Peafowl *(Pavo cristatus)*

life spared longer than normal, for the sake of safety and surety in rearing valuable pheasants. I mark my best hens with a bright red band on the right leg for each brood they raise. Some of them frequently receive two bands a year. The next best I mark with blue bands on the left leg. Thus, when I have valuable eggs and a selection of hens, I know which ones to use. I keep many of the hens until they die a natural death, even though they have long since stopped laying.

My experience has been that Silkies are the best foster mothers; they are both good setters and good mothers. They are easy to handle and, as a rule, are willing to take young birds that other hens have hatched. There are times when I must use larger hens; then I prefer the Rhode Island Red to any other breed. When the larger hens are used, they are set on the larger pheasant eggs, such as the Silver, Eared Pheasants and Impeyan. However, I would rather trust two Silkies with four eggs each than one Rhode Island Red with eight. At the end of the season the Silkies will have more to show for their season's work. It is true that the small hens don't cover as many eggs, but it is likewise true that they don't break as many or trample as many young to death. The Silky's greatest drawback is its feathered legs. Most of the feathers, however, may be clipped or removed by dipping in kerosene.

Bantams, Rhode Island Reds, Wyandottes and Plymouth Rocks usually make good foster mothers, but Leghorns, Anconas and Minorcas never should be used. The hen should be tested on china eggs for about forty-eight hours before she is given a setting of pheasant eggs.

When a number of hens are setting close quarters, be careful that they do not get mixed and sit on the wrong nests. This leads to trouble later. It is wise to mark or brand the hens in some way, either with a numbered leg band or by painting the hens' backs with the same number as on the nesting box.

CARE OF THE BROODY HEN

Feed and water the hen at a regular time each morning. Use scratch feed or whole corn (maize), with charcoal and grit. Turn down the upper half of the box and place the food in front of the hen. If, after you've waited a reasonable while and she has not come off at the sight of the food, remove her by placing your hand well back under her body, thus preventing her holding the eggs between her legs. Give her plenty to eat and drink and let her have a dust bath, if she will. Then put her back, if she does not go back by herself. Eggs can be exposed from fifteen to forty-five minutes, depending on the weather and the length of time they have been incubating. The first two days are the most critical period, as the embryo is just beginning to develop. The hen may be left off for about fifteen minutes the first week, twenty the second, and from twenty to thirty minutes the third, depending upon the weather. The warmer the weather and the longer they have been setting, the more exposure they will stand. If the weather is hot and dry, sprinkle the eggs with tepid water; also wet the earth around the setting box. Eggs from pheasants that live in hot, damp jungles need more moisture than eggs from those that live in high dry regions. I cannot advise you on how much moisture is needed, as this depends upon the weather as well as the build and location of the setting box. Each breeder must work this out for himself. Game pheasants' eggs are usually sprinkled with lukewarm water daily from the twenty-first day until they begin to pip. This should be done just before the hen is put back on the nest. In extremely dry weather, the eggs may be sprinkled two or three times before the twenty-first day.

Many young pheasants have been lost in the past and will be in the future if the hens are not properly dusted during the incubation period. If the following instructions are carefully followed, there is no reason why a single bird should be lost from lice, fleas or ticks.

If the rearing coop has been used before, it should be scraped and brushed clean of all debris. A pesticidal spray (follow the manufacturer's directions!) should be sprayed in the coop, with particular attention given to cracks and crevices. Be sure the coop is thoroughly dry before use. If kerosene or other volatile solutions are used, caution must be taken because of the fire hazard before the coops dried.

The hen should be dusted with a pesticidal powder before she is given the eggs and again on about the fifteenth day. Be sure that the whole bird is dusted, paying particular attention to the areas around the vent, on the hips, under the wings, on the neck and the

Lineated Kalij (*Lophura lineata*)

Bornean Crested Fireback (*Lophura ignita*)

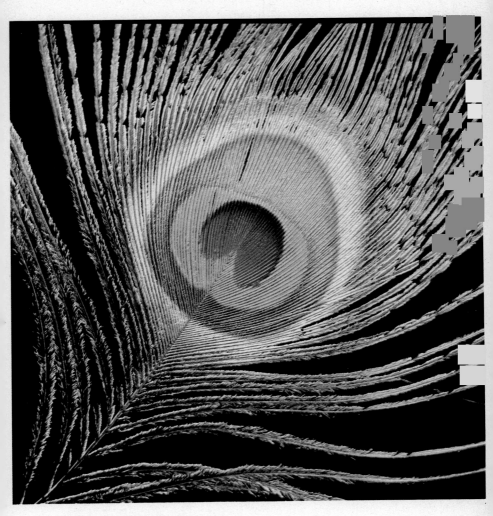

Detail of Peafowl tail feather

top of the head. Care must be taken not to get any of the dusting powder in the hen's eyes or nasal openings. *Do not use the liquid D.D.T. on birds or animals.*

Sodium flouride was formerly recommended, but in the light of more recent developments, it has been learned that other pesticides are safer to use and more effective, with longer lasting effects.

When eggs become broken, wash the rest of the eggs and the hen, using a rag and tepid water. Never leave soiled eggs in the nest, as the dry egg forms a film over the pores of the shell and smothers the embryo.

SETTING BOXES

My boxes for setting hens are built in pairs or twins so that they can be handled by one man. They are constructed of seven-eighths inch dressed lumber and are thirty-one inches long, fifteen inches wide, and fourteen inches high, with a partition in the center. The front is in two pieces; the upper section is ten inches, and the lower is four. The lower part is nailed fast, and the upper part is hinged to swing out. This allows the hen to step into the nest, instead of getting into it from the top, which might cause her to break some of the eggs. The top is separate but may be hinged in order to swing back to allow working in the nest. Ventilation may be provided by screening the door, or you may desire a solid door with a row of three-quarter inch holes bored around the top at both ends and in the back. The bottom is covered with half-inch hardware cloth, which is nailed to the outside. This wire permits the nesting material to touch the ground to absorb moisture. It also keeps rats and mice from burrowing under and annoying the hen. These setting boxes are readily moved about and can be stored in a small space when not in use. The above size is for Silkies and bantams only. For larger hens, the nest box should be about seventeen inches square. All nest boxes must be well ventilated, but they must have no holes through which the young pheasants might escape at hatching time. Boxes placed outside should be carefully fitted with a water-proof top.

Setting boxes can be built inside a building on a concrete floor. About four inches of moist soil must be placed in the box and a slightly concave nest depression hollowed out to receive the bedding. This earth must be kept sufficiently moist.

MAKING THE NEST

Lawn clippings, dry moss and broken straw make good nesting materials. Regardless of the material used, the nest should be one inch deep in the center and formed like a soup plate. If the nest is deeper, the eggs will pile up; if the nest is shallow, the eggs will roll out from under the hen and be chilled. Put a few drops of nicotine in the center of the nest. Fill all corners up even with the top of the nesting material. Be sure that there are no holes for the young to hide in; they are prone to run away and hide as soon as they are dry, thus becoming chilled. Young pheasants do not understand the hen's language and therefore must be confined close to the foster hen until they learn her call.

SETTING THE BROODY HEN

Because the broody hen plays an all-important part in the process of turning pheasant eggs into birds in the rearing of valuable species, and in small-scale production, extreme care must be taken

Nest box and feeding crate. The hinged weatherproof top of the nest box is thrown back and the screen door is open

Blue Peafowl *(Pavo cristatus)*

in choosing a hen. Handle her gently when placing her on the nest, which contains a few china or hard-boiled eggs, preferably at night, and leave her there for twenty-four hours. By that time, you can tell whether she means business or not; if not, leave her there for another day and night. Then, if she exhibits an inclination, give her the number of pheasant eggs she can comfortably cover, and make a note of the date and the kind of eggs. This record might be in the form of a journal, or it might be a notice tacked onto the inside of the nesting box lid. If you have eight valuable pheasant eggs, it is much better to evenly divide the eggs between two hens than to trust them all to one. When you have but two eggs to set, by reason of having only one pair of Argus or any of the Peacock Pheasants (both genera lay but two eggs to a clutch), it is best to add other eggs to offset and cause a more equal distribution of the hen's weight, thus greatly reducing the risk of breakage. To a setting of two Peacock Pheasant eggs, add four hard-boiled eggs of the same size. Golden Pheasant eggs also can be used. Bantam eggs are usually too large. To a setting of Argus eggs, add two medium-sized chicken eggs. Always use hard-boiled eggs, never dummy eggs made of china or other material harder than the shell of the real egg.

THE HATCH

When the little pheasants are breaking from their imprisoning shells, the amateur aviculturist is inclined to interfere. The experienced breeder leaves things absolutely alone. Nature has provided nourishment for the little birds for the next twenty-four hours, so you need have no worry in this respect. Leave the empty egg shells in the nest, as they help to offset the weight of the hen and protect the young from being mashed. Keep the setting box closed. If the weather is too hot to permit this, remove the top and cover with half-inch mesh hardware cloth. The cloth must fit snugly so the young won't escape, as many species are very wild when hatched. The Versicolors and Elliots are notorious for it, while the young Cheer, Eared Pheasants, Tragopans and Argus are as tame and as easy to handle as young chickens. For some unknown reason an occasional hen will kill the young as fast as they leave the shell; another will not molest them while in the nest but will kill them when placed in a nursery. But most hens make good foster mothers. However, when misfortune happens, it is

Newly hatched pheasant chicks in nursery coop, being kept warm by heat from lamp

best to mark the hen so that she won't be used again. Transfer the young to another hen, when possible making the transfer at night, because no hen takes kindly to strange birds. Silkies are very good in adopting motherless young.

No one knows exactly why hens kill the young, but this happens most frequently in hens that have not set a full incubating period. For example, when a hen that has been setting one week gets into a nest of eggs that will hatch in a day or so, she is not likely to make as good a foster mother as one that has set the full incubating period. Some hens seem to know that the little pheasants are foreigners, and they refuse to have anything to do with them, while others either do not know or do not care and mother them as though they were their own.

Those who have a small incubator often find it wise to remove pipped eggs from the hen and let the chicks hatch and dry in the machine, putting them back with the hen when it can be safely done.

THE NURSERY COOP

The purpose of this coop is to enable the breeder to control the young birds until they have learned the call of the foster mother and are ready to be placed in the field. They may be kept here from two to six days. When rarer species are involved, the coop should be sixteen by twenty-four by fourteen inches high, and should be constructed of light material (half-inch lumber is good). Half of the top might be covered with half-inch wire netting, the rest is a light wooden door; the floor to be of one-half inch hardware cloth, raised two inches from the bottom. The object of the wire netting is to permit the hen's droppings and waste food to drop through, out of reach of the birds, as well as preventing the hen from scratching and using the birds for a football. The smallest of the pheasants can run about the wire without injury. The covered top is to keep the birds in and rats and cats out. When hatched, the wings of most species of pheasants are well developed and they are able to fly when dry. It is better to have them under control than to be looking for them, as they hide well and it is hard to find them. Place the coop in a warm, dry place away from drafts, and see that the bottom fits tightly to the floor or ground to prevent underdrafts.

Before using the coop for another brood, it must be washed and sprayed with a disinfectant and placed in the sun to air and dry.

Several types of rearing coops may be used. The types that have proven best in tests with the more ordinary species, using commercially available equipment, are those having either a shed or "A"-type roof. These coops should be approximately thirty-six inches long, twenty inches wide and twenty-four inches high. The top and sides must be waterproof. Bars spaced three and one-half inches apart let the chicks range at will but still confine the hen to the coop.

Several days before the hatch is due, the coop should be placed on a level, well-drained spot from which all stubble and stone have been removed. Any tall grass within six feet of the coop should be cut to prevent the chicks from getting lost. Unless the wire-bottom coop is used, it is best to spread a burlap bag under the coop to keep the hen from scratching and killing the chicks. To help keep the chicks warm and dry in wet weather, tar paper may be placed under the burlap.

Brooder coop with run removed, equipped with feeder and water jar

Nursery coop with V-shaped run attached

A run is provided by attaching two boards thirty to thirty-six inches long and twelve inches high to the front of the coop in the form of a "**V**." It is very important that this run and coop be well banked with dirt to keep the chicks from getting out. They may be confined to this run for two or three days. This run is not advisable with the rarer species, because the chicks may be able to fly out of it. Of course, the coop must be put in a shaded—but not too cool—place.

To avoid chilling, it is best to move the chicks from the hatching box to the rearing coop between nine o'clock in the morning and two o'clock in the afternoon, the warmest part of the day. It is essential that the hen be well fed before being placed in the coop; otherwise, she is likely to do a great deal of scratching in search of food, possibly injuring the chicks.

While the hen is eating, the chicks should be kept in a warm place. They may be placed in a bushel basket, the bottom of which may be covered with excelsior. The top of the basket can be covered with a light cloth. After eating, the hen should be placed in the rearing coop with one or two chicks and given an opportunity to quiet down. The remainder of the chicks may then be placed in the coop with her. Do not disturb the hen for the next ten or twenty minutes, but after that it is advisable to quietly approach the coop to see whether the pheasants are being brooded by her. It is also important to check the coop the last thing in the evening to make certain that all chicks are underneath the hen; if they are not, slowly and gently place them underneath her by hand.

ARTIFICIAL INCUBATION

The artificial incubation of pheasants' eggs on game farms, where a large number of the same kind of eggs are available, has proved successful. But for the average breeder of fancy pheasants, incubators can be recommended provided that the breeder has the technique needed to handle an incubator.

Small incubators of the 100-egg capacity or smaller depend heavily upon the surrounding conditions. The proper balance of heat, humidity and ventilation can be gotten only in a small warm room, free from drafts and direct sunlight. Modern incubators are much easier to use than formerly was the case.

Until recently, game breeders used regular incubators of the small type which gave uneven heat above the eggs and little or no provision for moisture. Small units especially designed for game birds are available now, and dependable moisture regulation is provided. Proper operating conditions mean the difference between success and failure. The temperature of the air at the bottom of the egg is almost as important as the temperature reading of the thermometer level with the top of the egg. Most small units should operate in a room at 70-75 degrees F. When room temperature is dropped more than ten degrees at night, cooler air enters from below, cooling the bottom of the eggs, lowering the average temperature and resulting in poor hatches. Game birds, in particular, cannot develop properly if heat is not uniform.

Because small units need more attention, larger incubators are recommended when possible. The difference in good hatchability will pay for the extra cost over a period of years.

Results obtained by professional chicken hatchers to whom pheasant eggs are sent usually prove unsatisfactory. Some hatch, but the percentage has been so small that it has not been worth the effort. The birds develop but die in the shell, and the majority that do hatch are cripples.

The average breeder when desiring a large number of pheasants should find the results most satisfactory to set the necessary number of hens and then remove the young to brooders. Pheasants do well in brooders under treatment similar to that given chickens. However, some skillful breeders have gotten excellent results with small incubators. We use both kinds at Cleres.

ARTIFICIAL BROODING

Since the introduction of day-old chick distribution by some state agencies, the use of brooding equipment has become widespread. Many types have proved satisfactory. The Wisconsin Conservation Department has found that two distinct types of equipment best satisfy the various needs of breeders and sportsmen's groups.

SMALL BROODER HOUSE

This type is a small double brooder house with a screen porch; the dimensions are six feet long, seven feet wide and three feet high. The house is insulated throughout and has a combined capacity of 300 pheasant chicks.

Canopy style electric hover. Wire screen encircling hover keeps chicks confined; it should be arranged so it can be made larger as chicks grow. Cloth under hover must be changed daily

Brooders for the small double house can be of two small box-type electric brooders, or the small canopy type electric hover units, with at least a 500 watt heating unit. The capacity of each unit should be 150 chicks. The approximate size of the canopy type is twenty by thirty inches.

The brooder temperature should be regulated to maintain an even temperature of 100 degrees F. The current should be turned on twenty-four hours in advance of the arrival of the chicks, and the temperature should be re-checked to be absolutely sure that the temperature of the hover near the outside edge *on the floor* is ninety-five degrees. It is suggested that the thermometer be placed on the floor, because many commercial hovers have the thermometer extending from three to as high as six inches in the air.

Because of the location of the thermometer in the small double house, the temperature should be carried at 105 to 108 degrees, and the cutting of temperatures should be done very carefully about the third week, as sudden changes of temperature outside will change brooder temperatures.

Shelter pens and runs are required with both types of houses. Their size and construction have been discussed earlier in the book.

LARGE BROODER HOUSE

The other type recommended is the large house or an ordinary poultry brooder house. The dimensions of this house should be about twelve feet long, ten feet wide and six feet high. This house should also be insulated and properly ventilated. The brooder capacity of a house of this size is specified as being a 300-pheasant size.

Any type of commercial hover or canopy-style brooder may be used in the large house, either oil or electric. However, the use of coal brooders is not recommended. An electric brooder is usually depended upon to furnish a more uniform heat. The capacity of the hover must be at least 500-chick size.

Small double brooder house and shelter pen

Small double brooder house with door open showing data sheet—an essential when raising pheasant chicks. This type of brooder is designed to use with two small box-type brooders. It is divided to prevent crowding of chicks

PREPARATION OF EQUIPMENT

The brooder house should be thoroughly disinfected. Any commercial disinfectant is satisfactory. A very inexpensive solution consists of a small can of lye mixed with sixteen gallons of water. The house should be thoroughly scrubbed and allowed to dry out. The entire floor should then be covered with litter about two inches thick.

Any good litter, such as pine shavings (but not sawdust), peat moss or cotton seed hulls, can be used satisfactorily. Regardless of the type used, it must be spread over the whole floor about two inches thick. This will keep the chicks from scratching down to the floor where they find and eat small indigestible particles, which causes the gizzard to become impacted and results in starvation. If the small brooder house is used, the litter must be covered with a light colored cloth, preferably white, placed in front and extending one third of the way under the brooder.

If a canopy-type brooder is used, the entire space inside the circle used to confine the chicks to the brooder must be covered

137

with cloth or rough paper. Regardless of type of brooder used, the cloth should be continued for five or six days and changed daily.

Sprinkle a generous amount of chick feed on the cloth and place at least five small chick feeders and five two-quart jar-type fountains inside the circle for the large type brooder, and two of each in the small type. After five or six days, discontinue the cloth and circle. At this time, the feeders and fountains should be placed on two frames made of one-by-four-inch lumber and covered with half-inch hardware cloth. These are later used in the shelter pens described previously in the book.

In order that the chicks be confined close to the hover, a screen should be used in the small type house and placed approximately six inches from the brooder. The canvas flap in front of the box brooder should be about two inches from the cloth on the floor to allow the chicks a free run to and from the brooder. This is discontinued after the first day, and chicks are allowed the entire brooder house space.

In the case of the canopy-type brooder, an ordinary screen or guard consisting of either cardboard or half-inch mesh wire about twelve inches in width should be placed approximately six inches to a foot away from the brooder proper so that the chicks cannot wander too far away from the heat. This screen or guard should be made so that the chicks can be made larger as the chicks grow older.

When the chicks are two weeks old, they may go outside early in the morning, when weather permits, but they should be driven back into the house at night. Gradually move the waterers and feeders outside. Supply plenty of green food, shade and cover.

When the birds are eight to ten weeks old, they may be transferred to holding pens or shelters or stocked in the wild.

HEALTH MEASURES

Pheasants are subject to many of the diseases and parasites common to poultry. Little difficulty should be experienced in the raising of pheasants if certain procedures are followed.

Always keep clean, dry litter in the brooder house. This is a very essential rule to follow, because moldy litter contains spores that are inhaled by the young birds. The spores in turn not only produce a gangrenous necrotic (wasting away) pneumonia but also develop in the air sacs, eventually resulting in death. Infections of nearly any nature may arise from unsanitary conditions. Such conditions also promote the development of parasites. Concentration of birds in a given area means parasitism. Following strict measures with special regard to the litter will prevent these conditions.

Keep an even temperature and do not chill or overheat the birds. Avoid drafts. The exposure of the young pheasants to variations in temperature and drafts can be readily seen on post-mortem examination. The lung is no longer the normal rosy-pink color, but in many cases becomes bluish and solidified. Many of the birds die from exposure. Although some of them may have enough resistance to live, traces of pneumonia may be seen throughout the life of the birds; there is a permanent injury to the lung tissue.

Both animal and bird life have a means of making the best of these injuries by completely sealing off the offending abscess. This later becomes a hard calcified mass. From this it can be seen that the area of functioning lung is greatly reduced.

During cold, damp seasons, many young pheasants die from pneumonia. This is the easiest of all the conditions to control, because it requires merely a constant regulation and watching of the brooder temperature. During spring weather, the birds get wet and then do not dry out thoroughly; if they are exposed to drafts, they contract pneumonia.

Do not let chicks range on ground contaminated by poultry. Since the pheasant is susceptible to many of the diseases and parasites of chickens, this must be kept in mind. Coccidia, according to recent research, seem to be the worst offenders. The mortality is high, and the birds die within a week. This occurs mostly in birds from one to three weeks of age. Some of them survive, but they do not respond to good wholesome food or treatment.

General sanitation, including movement of coops and movement of breeder houses and runs insofar as it is possible, is recommended in the prevention of blackhead and coccidiosis. Liming the soil followed by plowing or spading will help to decrease the infestation found in the soil. However, after several generations of birds have used the same ground, it can hardly be expected that disease and parasite-free birds can be raised as successfully as birds raised on new and uncontaminated ground.

Place feed and water on wire frames and disinfect hoppers and water fountains frequently. This procedure is also essential; the young birds will pass droppings into the water and feed, thereby exposing the rest of the flock to parasites and diseases. The eggs of these parasites are not visible to the naked eye; they may be seen only with the aid of a microscope.

Any chlorine disinfectant used for cleaning milk utensils may be used to disinfect hoppers and water fountains. The action of chlorine is powerful, and it has an affinity for hydrogen, thereby separating the oxygen from the water. Oxidation, of course, destroys organic matter. Bacteria and parasite eggs are either destroyed or injured to the extent that they are no longer active. No odor is left by the disinfectant during this process. This is quite important, as in many cases birds will not eat foods that have offensive odors.

Do not make any sudden change in the birds' rations. This not

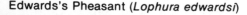
Edwards's Pheasant (*Lophura edwardsi*)

only throws the birds off feed but also, in some instances, will readily show up as a disturbance in nutrition.

Remove the chill from all water given chicks. In the summer this is done by the sun in a very few minutes. It is also well to add sufficient potassium permanganate (the amount held on a dime per gallon of water) as a drinking water disinfectant. This does not mean that the water may be left and not changed; the water must be changed twice daily.

Provide plenty of shade and shelter, because birds are more contented in cool shaded places, especially during the hot weather.

Guard against cannibalism. Cannibalism may develop during any stage in the life of the young pheasants. However, the desire to dominate becomes more assertive in birds from two to three weeks old.

Should cannibalism occur during the first week of rearing, check the temperature of the brooder to see that it is not too high. Sup ply more feeding hoppers and darken the brooder house; if necessary, use ruby lights. It would be best to keep juicy green food before them. Lawn clippings, chopped lettuce and chopped alfalfa are good sources of Vitamin A. A lack of this is believed to be one of the causative factors.

Should cannibalism develop after the third week, it may be cured by providing plenty of brush within the large pen so that they may escape from one another. It is best to remove all picked birds and apply pine tar to the affected parts.

Do not try to rear birds of different ages in the same pen, as this induces cannibalism.

MODERN METHODS

Since the last edition of this book appeared (1953), important new methods of keeping and breeding pheasants have developed. They are designed to make things simpler and to save labor, and they can be summarized as follows:

Feeding

Scientifically composed pellets and crumbs have largely replaced freshly mixed foods. They are generally very satisfactory and much easier to distribute, both to adult and to young birds, according to season. A number of appropriate foods exist to suit the different species. Some also contain drugs against various diseases.

They do not, however, completely replace green and live foods, which remain essential to a number of delicate species.

Incubation

Techniques of egg incubation and chick rearing have considerably changed. Proper handling of eggs before incubation, particularly sterilization of the shells in dip solutions, has improved chances of successful storage. The best temperature for stored eggs is 50-60°F, with 50-70% humidity.

Brooding hens require a lot of time-consuming care, and they also can be disease carriers. They are at present increasingly replaced by the much-improved incubators and brooders currently on the market. There are many excellent types now available; with proper management, a maximum of 80% success is expected.

Rearing Pheasants

A successful rearing system for the small breeder is the non-confinement plan under which the pheasant chicks are closely confined for the first two or three days, after which the run is removed and they are given free range. The hen is not permitted to run with the chicks. It is important that the coop be shifted to clean ground every day.

The confinement system is recommended in all cases where the birds are being reared in backyards and other localities where predatory birds and animals cannot be controlled. The hen, as in the non-confinement plan, is kept in the rearing coop at all times, but after the small V-shaped run has been removed, the chicks are given the run of a pen approximately twelve feet long, four feet wide and from five to six feet high. A door large enough to admit one person should be made in this pen. The base of the pen should be boarded up to a height of from one to one and a half feet; the balance of the pen, including the top, should be covered with three-quarter or one-inch mesh wire. To avoid the danger of diseases resulting from contaminated ground, and to give the young chicks an ample supply of green food, the pen should be so made that it may be moved at frequent intervals.

REARING FIELD, RUN AND COOP

Aviculturists rearing the rarer species will prefer a slightly more elaborate rearing coop and run that may easily be moved about by two men. The run may be six feet wide, ten or twelve feet long and two feet, eight inches high; the framing, seven-eighths by three inches; the uprights, two by two inches; and it should be constructed of dressed cypress. The brood coop should be three inches above the ground to prevent dampness and should be attached to one end of the run on the outside.

The top of the run is covered with one-inch mesh poultry netting and the coop end, for one-half of the distance, should be covered with roofing paper over the poultry netting. This protects the birds from the sun and rain. The sides are covered with two-mesh-to-the-inch hardware cloth, fastened one inch up on the top of the frame. This will leave an overhang of six inches at the bottom. In use, this overhang is pegged or loaded down with sod or earth to prevent the birds from getting under. Each end should have a door large enough to work through. The brood coop is twenty-four inches square, the front being twenty-two inches high and the rear nineteen inches, with the roof extending four inches in the back to let the rain drip clear. Ventilation comes from the wire-covered opening at the top, on both sides and the front. The bottom must be tight, to prevent drafts and to hold the floor covering when in use. There is a sliding door in the front to let the hen enter. This door is made so that it can be opened and closed from without, with another opening in the side. This opening must be large enough so that a person can place both arms inside at the same time, as pheasants must be grasped with both hands to prevent injury. The opening at the coop end of the run is for feeding purposes, while the door at the opposite end is to permit the transferring of birds from one run to another without handling. To transfer birds, confine them first to one brood coop, then place the ends of two runs together, open the doors of both runs—and free the birds from the coop—and soon they will exchange themselves without handling, saving time, fright, and the risk of injury.

When the birds no longer require brooding, place a roost crosswise of the run, two feet above the ground and under the roof. The roost must not be in the sun as long as the birds require brooding. If it is placed there too soon, the hen will go to roost and leave the birds unprotected, inviting colds, croup, etc.

THE REARING FIELD

The rearing field coops are best placed on a hillside facing south. Put the runs near the foot of the grade and work uphill, thus preventing any wash of filth, which occurs when runs are started at the top and worked down. Set the runs over a previously prepared dust bath, and see that the overhanging wire is securely pegged or loaded down to prevent the birds' escape. Be very careful about this, because birds have escaped even when great care is taken. Cover the coop floor with two inches of dry grass or

Young pheasants in open pens must have their wings clipped. Note the way the bird is held for the clipping procedure

broken straw; during very hot weather, cover the roof of the coop with grass or hay to keep out the heat.

For chicks of some species that are easily infected, it is best to keep them off the soil in runs with wire netting floors raised above the ground. This precaution should be taken for the first few weeks, until after the end of the first molt.

Fixed rearing pens with concrete floors can be used also. It is well to lay a few inches of peat on the concrete, which should be slightly pitched in order to drain. This peat must be changed often, and the floor should be disinfected. The birds should be removed during these operations.

In case the birds are not confined in a pen having a covered top, it will be necessary to clip them after they are two weeks old. After that, they must be clipped every two weeks until three weeks before the time they are to be freed or housed in covered shelter. At this time the stub feathers should be pulled; if they are not, full growth of new feathers won't be insured. However, if the birds are clipped only once, it will not be necessary to pull the stub feathers. In case the confinement plan is used, a landing net may be used in catching the birds, and care should be taken not to hurt them. In removing the birds from the net, grasp them by both legs.

When the young pheasants are from five to seven weeks old, they will begin to leave the hen. She may be then removed. Shelter, as well as the coop, should also be given.

If the birds are being raised to be freed, it should be noted that young birds can care for themselves between ten and fourteen

Comparison of flight feather growth at weekly intervals

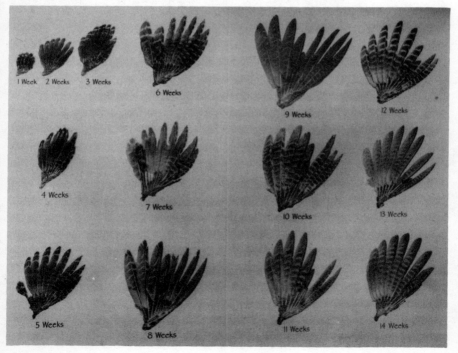

weeks. However, age is not always the determining factor. Young pheasants shouldn't be released until good judgment tells you that they can well care for themselves.

CARE OF THE YOUNG

You can place the grit, food and water either inside the run door at the coop end or inside the coop. By placing the food inside the coop, the birds get used to feeding there, and when it's time to close up for the night they will enter for their evening meal. Otherwise, they must be driven in, as they must stay in the coop at night—at least until they are fully feathered. In the coop they are safe from weasels, skunks, etc. Too many precautions cannot be taken. When the young do not need to be brooded, the hen should be taken away, as many troubles come directly from her—the sooner the source of contamination is removed, the better. The coop should be moved to fresh ground when the grass is gone, which will be in about another week. If the birds don't do as well as they should, the coop should be moved to another part of the field and examined for lice; lice make the birds weak and susceptible to disease. Birds with lice do not grow as they should. When lice are found, both the hen and birds should be treated. Remove the litter and burn it. Change the diet and look for worms in the excrement. Spray the coop with a five percent carbolic acid solution, driving the solution well into the cracks, and keep the birds outside until the coop is thoroughly dry.

ARTIFICIAL REARING OF PHEASANTS

Regardless of where the chicks come from, your incubator or the state agency, the brooder should be operating and at a 100 degree F. temperature at least twenty-four hours before the chicks come. Litter, as prescribed, should cover the entire floor of the brooder house, and white cloth should be placed in front of the brooder and in or around the hover, depending upon the type of brooder unit used. Starting feed should be sprinkled liberally on the cloth. A supply of lukewarm water should be available together with a number of one- or two-quart jars with pebbles in the trough.

When the chicks arrive, they should be put underneath the brooder or hover. In most cases, many of them will start eating right away. If the temperature is correct, they will seem very active. Watering jugs can then be placed in front of the brooder or around the hover.

If the small double house is used, the chicks should have about six inches of space directly in front of the brooder. After the first day, the screen is put on top of the brooder to keep the chicks from getting up on the brooder. They can be given the run of the space afforded by the screen or cardboard guard, but you should enlarge the space daily as explained above. Always check temperatures carefully.

When using a canopy-type brooder, the screen or guard that encircles the hover will confine the chicks close enough to the heat. The screen necessary for the small unit should be used the first twenty-four hours, after which the chicks actually learn to find the heat and will brood properly. With the canopy-type brooder, however, you will find that they will brood properly if they aren't too closely confined. It is good to check the brooder the last thing every night until the chicks stop using it, because they often leave the brooder and pile into the corners.

The small double house has a screen porch, and after the fifth day, if the weather is good, the chicks may use the porch. When the chicks do, one of the two feeders and waterers from inside should be placed on the porch. Chicks, however, should be driven in at night for the first two or three days, and the door of the house closed. This door should be opened early in the morning.

In a larger brooder house, the screen or guard can be completely removed and the chicks given free run of the entire house. If chicks are eating from hoppers, the cloth can be removed—but all must be eating before this is done.

If the chicks are to be confined in the brooder house after the cloth bags are no longer used, the small feeders and waterers should be placed on a half-inch mesh wire screen until they are allowed the use of the shelter pen.

If the weather is very mild after the tenth day, the chicks may be permitted to use the shelter pen. They, however, must be driven back into the house at night. They must be taught to go to and from the shelter pen to the house before all doors can be left open. Large feeders and waterers should be out in the shelter pen at this time, and they should be put up off the ground on a wire screen so

Vulturine Guineafowl (*Acryllium vulturinum*)

that the birds don't eat wet or moldy feed.

At two weeks, the pheasants are usually able to use the large run. They should be driven into the twelve by twelve shelter pens every night until they are from four to five weeks old. The doors to the brooder house or porch should be left open so that if a storm comes the birds can be driven into the shelter pen.

When the chicks are three weeks old, the temperature under the hover should be lowered gradually at the rate of five degrees per week. The temperature should also be regulated according to the birds' actions. If they tend to pile up, they are too cold; if they pant, and their wings are droopy, it is too hot.

At four weeks, the starting mash can be replaced gradually with a growing mash. Feed hoppers should be kept filled, and an ample supply of fresh water should be available, in as many places as possible. Many feeders and waterers do away with congregating, and this will eliminate a tendency toward cannibalism. A quantity of grit, charcoal and oyster shells also should be supplied. When all the green food has been consumed within the shelter pen, it is best to lime the soil and turn over the sod. Brush can be added in the shelter pens.

During the sixth week, a small amount of grain may be added to the feed. This can be increased gradually until the ration consists of one-fourth grain, three-fourths mash.

When the birds are from six to ten weeks old, they won't have to be driven into the shelter pen. Some of them will roost out in the large pens, and therefore additional shelters should be provided for this purpose. In the event of a damp, rainy season, it is best not to let the cover crops in the large runs become too thick.

If the birds are being reared for liberation, they usually can be released from the tenth to fourteenth week, depending on their physical condition. However, it should be remembered that birds should not be released until fully feathered, i.e., full tail feathers and full wing feathers, and they *must be able to care for themselves.*

In case the large runs aren't covered, it would be necessary to pull the feathers of clipped birds three weeks before they are to leave. Full growth of wing feathers usually can occur within that time. However, if the birds were clipped only once, then stub feathers need not be pulled.

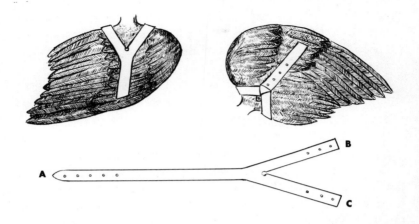

Diagram of brail and proper method of attaching it. Top left, under-side of wing. Top right, outside of wing. Bottom: brail

CLIPPING AND BRAILING

When catching birds for clipping, an ordinary landing net may be used, and care must be taken not to hurt the birds. When using a net, let the birds run into the net. In taking them out, grasp the birds by both legs. This is very important, because their legs are easily broken. Hold the bird securely, the two legs between the third and little fingers, place the thumb over the head of the bird and spread the wing with the index finger and the thumb. Then clip the first eight flight feathers with ordinary scissors. *It is not necessary to clip the wing too closely.*

INSTRUCTIONS FOR BRAILING

A pheasant brail is a leather strap that measures approximately eight and one-half inches in length and one-half inch in width. One end of the brail is split. The brail is made of very soft leather so as not to injure the wing of the bird. Brails may be split down about one and one-half inches from the end. They may be made by the user or purchased inexpensively enough. It is not advisable to attempt to brail young pheasants.

Take the split ends of the brail and pass them around the shoulder of the bird so that the ends meet at the top of the shoulder. Take the long end and slip it between the first and second flight feathers, bringing it around to meet the split ends. Adjust the brail to allow the wing about half play, but not enough for proper flight. Fasten the three ends with a brass split pin with prongs facing out.

If birds are penned for a long period, brails must be changed from one wing to another every three weeks to one month.

INSTRUCTIONS FOR PULLING STUB FEATHERS

Use a landing net to catch birds and take great care not to injure them. Grasp them by both legs when removing them from the net. Hold the bird with its head toward you and spread the wing with the thumb and first finger of the same hand. Use pliers or the fingers to pull the stub feather upward. Care should be taken not to pull a blood or blue feather because this may induce bleeding and cannibalism may develop. Blue or blood feathers grow more rapidly than others. If you have clipped the bird properly, you should experience no trouble.

Pheasant Health
And Disease Control

Both the pheasant fancier and the commercial pheasant breeder recognize the fact that profitable production depends upon pheasant health. By and large, pheasants are among the healthiest domesticated birds, and observance of a few common sense rules will contribute to maintaining this favorable status. Modern disease control does not wait for sickness to strike—it utilizes the available knowledge on prevention by sanitation, vaccination and medication. The intelligent application of this knowledge is based upon the accurate recognition of the various diseases affecting pheasants. Such recognition can be achieved only by means of laboratory diagnoses of all or most of the losses. Injury is relatively common in pheasants and, if not resulting in immediate death, may simulate paralytic diseases. The summation of diagnoses over a period of time will inform the pheasant breeder as to the principal disease troubles prevalent on his premises or in the particular area and enable him to plan an effective disease-prevention program. By making daily observations on the health of the flock, by keeping accurate mortality records and by submitting, in cases of sickness, suitable specimens to a diagnostic laboratory, the pheasant breeder becomes the key man in maintaining the health of a pheasant flock.

Planning For Disease Prevention. If one has the choice, much can be done in the line of disease prevention by proper planning of the premises. Since pheasants are subject to many of the same diseases as domesticated poultry the premises should be isolated as much as possible. The houses should be well constructed to give shelter and to lend themselves to periodic clean-up and disinfection. The fly pens should be well drained and suitable for rotation, plowing, harrowing and reseeding in case of soil-borne diseases.

It is best to have only one bird species on the premises because species other than pheasants, although not obviously susceptible to certain diseases, may still act as disease carriers and thus contribute to perpetuating the trouble. For similar reasons brooding and growing operations should be widely separated from the breeding stock. Preventive measures will be discussed later.

Submitting Specimens for Laboratory Diagnosis. Every pheasant breeder should know the location of the nearest diagnostic laboratory, also the veterinarians and feed service men on whom he can call for help. As a rule, live, typically affected pheasants are needed for complete laboratory examination. If dead specimens are also taken to the laboratory one must make certain that they

A gross post mortem examination is one way to diagnose pheasant and other poultry disease

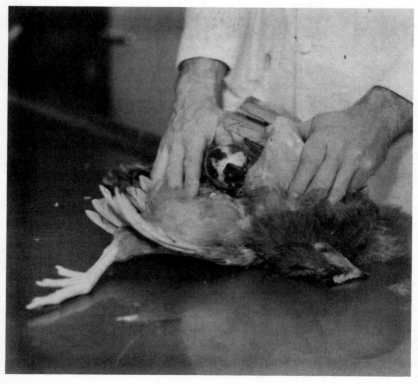

have died on the day of submission. In addition detailed mortality records should be furnished, in the case of brooder chicks on a day-by-day basis.

The Classification of Disease. The principal differentiation of diseases and disorders is on the basis of their cause, mainly nutritional and infectious in nature. Ordinarily the pheasant breeder is not interested in detailed descriptions of causative organisms; on the other hand, it is of practical importance to him to be familiar with the main differences among groups of infectious agents in order to know their probable mode of spread and the best means of combatting them. As a rule, the smaller the infectious agent, the easier it can spread. For purposes of description causative organisms may be arranged according to their size.

Internal parasites (worms in almost every case) may live in the intestine, windpipe, and so forth. They are usually visible with the unaided eye.

Protozoans are one-celled animals of microscopic size.

Fungi or **molds** are many-celled plants. Only a few of the common molds have disease-producing properties. Massive colonies of fungi such as common bread molds are often visible.

Bacteria or **germs** are one-celled plants of microscopic size.

Pleuropneumonia-like organisms and the **Rickettsia** group stand intermediate between bacteria and true viruses, and are sometimes called large viruses. They are barely visible under the optical microscopic and, as a rule, non-filterable. The former can be cultivated on artificial media, whereas this has not been accomplished with *Rickettsia*.

Viruses form a large complex group of organisms which are filterable through bacteria-retaining filters and invisible under all but the most powerful electron optical microscopes. In other words, their existence is detected primarily by what they can do to susceptible animals (or plants) in the type of disease they can induce. Viruses cannot be cultivated artificially, except in the presence of living cells.

The following discussion of pheasant diseases based upon their cause is not exhaustive but aims to present the principal ailments of practical importance. To assist the pheasant breeder in arriving at a probable diagnosis from flock observations, a table of pheasant diseases, arranged according to outward signs, will be found in Appendix I.

NUTRITIONAL DISEASES

Under practical conditions few nutritional disorders occur. This does not mean that the feeding of artificially reared pheasants can not be improved, especially for the purposes of meat production.

While it would be possible for the fancier to compound his own feed according to available nutritional formulas, the commercial pheasant breeder may do well to utilize the services of a feed company which prepares special feeds for pheasants and other game birds and has the opportunity to conduct supervised feeding trials. A satisfactory practice is to start with feed in mash form and to switch to small pellets within a few weeks.

White streaking of the breast and leg muscles is observed in apparently normal pheasants. Scientifically the condition is indistinguishable from muscular dystrophy of ducklings maintained on a vitamin E-deficient diet. Although this pheasant condition has not been observed to bring about obvious sickness, it is conceivable that the muscle lesions impair the capacity to fly and the appearance of the carcass.

PARASITIC DISEASES

Among the diseases caused by external or internal parasites, the most important one is gapeworm disease, brought about by infection of the windpipe with the roundworm *Syngamus trachea*.

Chickens, turkeys, guinea-fowl, geese and various wild birds are likewise susceptible and capable of passing the disease to pheasants.

The female worm is up to three-quarters inch in length and bright red when fresh, the male about one-quarter inch. The sexes are attached and form the letter **"Y."** The worm eggs are ordinarily coughed up, swallowed and passed out in the feces. Larvae hatching from the eggs in a favorable environment undergo several moltings and then become infective to pheasants or encyst in earthworms, slugs, snails and flies. Thus the ground may become contaminated for years.

The ingested larvae migrate from the intestine through the lung to the windpipe. Young birds (except young turkeys, which are primarily carriers) suffer most from gapeworm infection. Symptoms appear about fourteen days after ingestion of infective larvae and are respiratory in nature, from gasping to actual suffocation.

Treatment of affected birds may be tried on an individual basis by removing the worms with a stripped feather from, or by instilling a few drops of Iodine Vermicide Merck in, the trachea. Small-scale group treatment may be carried out by dusting the birds in a box with barium antimonyl tartrate. This product, however, is not commercially available and has to be especially prepared. A proprietary compound sold under the name "Blackerite" by Spratts Patent, Newark, N.J. is said to give good results, according to Grant (1958).

Bacteriologic examination being performed to find disease-causing germs

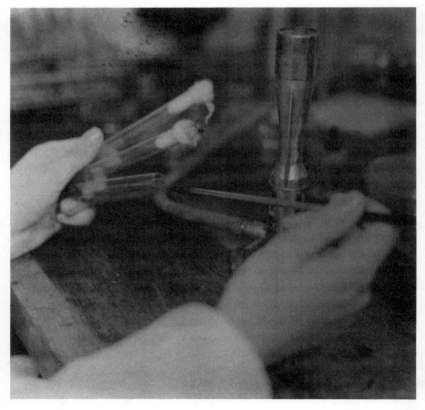

Prevention of gapeworm disease by continuous feedings of three to four percent phenothiazine in the mash has been reported in England. Since the drug is used at six to eight times the ordinary dose (0.5%) for the treatment of cecal worms, it must be used with caution. Before flock treatment, the drug should be tried on a few birds. Another approach is through soil sanitation, to reduce the earthworm population. The most effective chemical has been found to be the Shell D-D which is applied to the soil with a spot injector available from the same outlets as the chemical. Soil treatment should usually start with the brooder pens. A cover of coarse gravel may also be used. Even eradication of earthworms may not completely eliminate the disease.

If the disease is a major problem, it is advisable to consult with the respective official state game board. Helpful information can also be obtained from Bulletin 315 (1955) "Control of the Gapeworm in the Ring-Necked Pheasant in Connecticut" by M.R. Anderson and J. Shapiro, Storrs Agricultural Experiment Station, Storrs, Conn., and "Profitable Game Management" by D.T. Grant, The Beacon Milling Co., Caygua, N.Y., 9th Ed. (1958).

PROTOZOAN DISEASES

Like most other domesticated birds, pheasants suffer occasionally from coccidiosis. The organisms live in the intestinal surface cells for about a week and then pass out in the droppings and undergo further development before becoming reinfective. The intensity of the disease depends primarily on the number of infective organisms and on a favorably warm and moist environment, especially in the litter. Mild infections are harmless and induce immunity to subsequent infections with the same coccidial species, of which there are two, *Eimeria phasiani*, which affects pheasants alone, and *Eimeria dispera*, which affects also quail.

Preventive treatment in the feed with sulfaquinoxaline or other drugs—as used in chickens—is usually not necessary. For emergency water medication, sodium sulfaquinoxaline or sulfamethazine is available.

Blackhead is another protozoan disease, caused by *Histomonas meleagridis*. The disease also affects turkeys, grouse, peacocks and occasionally chickens; it brings about loose yellow droppings, large cheesy blind guts and cartwheel-like depressions in the liver.

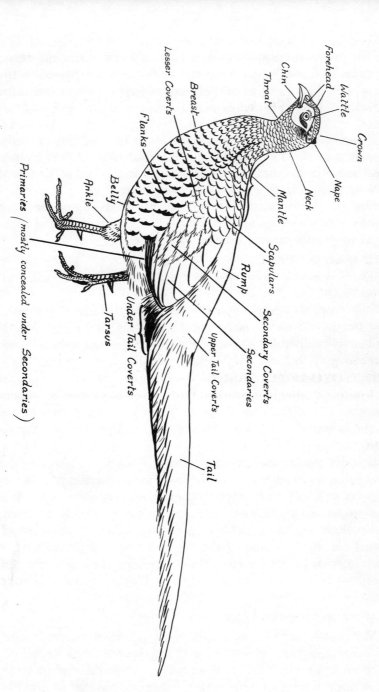

Diagram defining the external parts of a pheasant

The protozoan organism often enters the egg of the pin worm, commonly living in the blind gut of fowl. When passed in the feces, it is able to live in infected soil for several years, even in the absence of birds. Chickens and other species act as blackhead carriers.

Preventive and curative treatments have recently become available in the form of urazolidone (NF-180). Unless trouble from blackhead recurs, curative treatment in the feed at the rate of two or three pounds per ton should be used.

For short-term treatment the therapeutic feeds compounded for chickens or turkeys and often containing furazolidone and high-level antibiotics may be used to advantage.

FUNGAL DISEASES

There are two conditions in this group primarily affecting brooder chicks.

` Sour crop, also called thrush or moniliasis, is caused by a yeast-like fungus, *Candida albicans,* that affects a wide variety of birds and occasionally man. The inside of the crop shows slightly raised circular grayish foci, which become confluent and form loosely adherent membranes. The organism is hardy and has been known to live on dry wood for over ten years. Treatment may be attempted with 1:2000 (one-half teaspoonful per gallon) copper sulphate in the drinking water, but ultimate control depends upon sanitation.

Brooder pneumonia or aspergillosis is caused by *Aspergillus fumigatus,* a common mold which may cause chronic pneumonia in birds and mammals, including man. Since the lungs of birds communicate with the air sacs, the latter may present greenish-blue colonies, gasping and high mortality. Adult pheasants so affected become thin and finally die. No treatment is known for such internal fungal diseases. Moldy litter may be responsible for the disease in chicks and should be avoided. General sanitation must be relied upon for adult disease control.

BACTERIAL DISEASES

Most of the bacterial diseases of pheasants are shared with other domesticated birds, which fact is of importance in transmission.

Navel ill, or omphalitis, is a bacterial infection caused by a variety of germs which enter through the unhealed navel at or near hat-

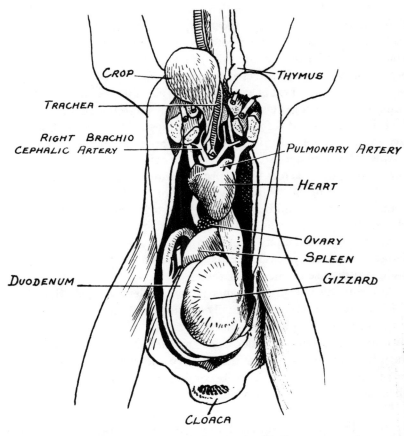

Diagram showing viscera; ventral aspect with liver removed

ching time. Affected chicks suffer high mortality during the first seven to ten days of brooding. On opening, they present a "belly button" or encrusted navel under the abdominal skin and, on the inside, large unabsorbed egg yolk with thick, crumbly, occasionally foul-smelling content. The control is entirely a matter of incubator sanitation. Before setting eggs, the incubator should be subjected to cleaning and triple-strength formalinization (one ounce formaldehyde and one-half ounce potassium permanganate per 100 cubic feet of incubator space). In severe cases the latter procedure may have to be repeated at hatching time.

Pullorum disease, or bacillary white diarrhea, caused by *Salmonella pullorum,* is the most important bacterial disease and entirely preventable by the methods outlined in the disease control phase of the National Poultry Improvement Plan. The causative organism passes from infected females (or males) through the egg to the chicks, in which it causes heavy mortality. At time of hatching the organism is also disseminated through the air in forced-draft incubators and through the droppings in the brooder house. According to the infective cycle, control is based upon blood-testing the breeder stock before using hatching eggs, and eliminating the reactors. This process should be continued until an official rating of "Pullorum Clean" or "Pullorum Passed" is obtained. Eggs should be incubated only together with eggs from pheasants or other birds of like or better "pullorum status." As pheasant egg incubation is often a specialty job, there is a real danger of clean pheasant eggs becoming contaminated with pullorum disease in the incubator.

Pullorum disease in pheasants is usually less virulent than in chickens and therefore more easily overlooked. This fact should be a stimulus to the pheasant breeder, rather than a deterrent, to clean up this disease in a flock once and for all, for the benefit of the pheasant industry and the poultry industry at large. State game departments are also becoming insistent on liberating pheasants only from known pullorum-clean stock.

The signs in affected chicks are nonspecific. They consist of whitish diarrhea and unusual mortality during the second and third week of brooding. On opening a dead bird, one might find enlargement of liver and tiny grayish nodules in heart and lung. Egg-producing hens may present malformed "blighted" follicles in the ovary and heart nodules. The diagnosis in all cases rests upon bacteriologic demonstration of the causative organism. Temporary treatment of affected chicks may be tried with furazolidone (as for blackhead) but is advisable only if the survivors are not intended for breeding purposes.

Fowl typhoid, caused by *Salmonella gallinarum,* has many similarities with pullorum disease but tends to affect growing and adult birds. On opening the liver presents a characteristic dark brown color with a metallic greenish sheen; the spleen is often enlarged.

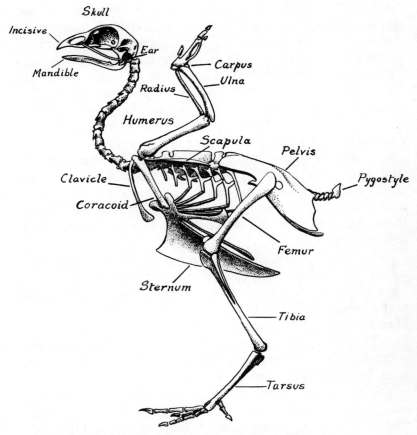

Diagram of the skeletal structure of the pheasant.

Chronic disease carriers can be detected by the standard blood test for pullorum disease and should be eliminated.

Paratyphoid, or salmonellosis, is caused by a large group of bacteria closely related to those of pullorum disease and fowl typhoid, except that true paratyphoid organisms are motile. Paratyphoid organisms occur throughout the higher animal kingdom, including snakes, with birds constituting the principal reservoir. In pheasants the disease acts very much like navel ill, except that it is caused by a specific paratyphoid germ and is subject to similar control measures, including furazolidone treatment, as indicated.

Fowl cholera, caused by *Pasteurella multocida*, is one of the oldest known diseases of domesticated birds. It usually attacks grown birds in an acute or chronic form. In the first instance, the disease may be so virulent that birds apparently healthy in the morning die from it in the afternoon. Such acutely affected birds fail to show significant signs or lesions. Birds lingering with the disease for a few days present evidence of pneumonia and yellow exudate over the ovarian follicles (peritonitis). The chronic form often affects the middle ear or other parts of the head and may be accompanied by swelling or twisting of the neck.

Emergency treatment of the acute form may be attempted with 0.04 percent sodium sulfaquinoxaline in the drinking water, but must be accompanied by moving healthy birds to clean ground, away from stagnant water pools. Chronic cases are carriers and should be eliminated. If fowl cholera is recurrent in the flock, depopulation is advised.

Tuberculosis is caused by the avian type of *Mycobacterium tuberculosis*, which affects birds and swine. Tuberculosis is a disease of mature birds, and, unless breeding stock is carried over into the next season, rarely constitutes a problem. On the other hand, pheasants are highly susceptible to the infection and may be afflicted by this chronic disease in areas where poultry tuberculosis is rampant. For the same reason importation of mature breeding stock from foreign countries may be dangerous.

The symptoms of tuberculosis are diarrhea and progressive wasting away leading to death. Of the internal organs the spleen is first affected by the formation of grayish projecting nodules which also appear in the liver and lung. Occasionally these nodules mat into a solid mass.

Although there is a skin test and blood test available for the detection of avian tuberculosis, the procedure is usually disappointing, because new reactors may be found on successive tests. In severe cases, depopulation is advisable. The premises may be restocked with pheasant chicks after competent cleaning and disinfection.

Limberneck, or botulism, is really not a bacterial infection but a poisoning due to a toxin produced by *Clostidium botulinum*. Several subtypes of this germ are known to cause botulism in man and animals, type C being commonly involved in pheasants. The botulinus toxin is one of the most powerful toxins known and may occur in spoiled sausages, cans of food, hay and other decomposing organic matter. For emergency treatment high priced commercial antitoxin is available, but it is effective only against the specific type involved, and this in the early stages of the disease.

In pheasants botulism may occur either in individual birds or as a veritable epizootic, particularly in the summer. It is likely that an individual pheasant gets the disease from decomposing matter, insects having ingested such decomposing matter, or bacterial spores from the soil; the first succumbing bird may then serve as a source of infection for other birds and spread the disease.

As the common name limberneck implies, affected birds become weak in the legs or wings, prostrate and unable to hold up the neck. The cloaca is often distended by a dry or liquid mixture of feces and urine. The internal organs are normal. A definite diagnosis requires demonstration of the botulinus toxin by mouse inoculation with liver extract and neutralization with specific antitoxin.

Emergency treatment with antitoxin is expensive and not highly rewarding. It is best to isolate the affected birds as soon as possible and to put them on a straight milk diet. The first step in the control is to rid the premises of decomposing materials, including dead birds hidden in tall vegetation, and to move the healthy birds to clean ground. For long-range control, especially on problem farms, it is best to provide for pen rotation and reseeding of plowed pens with some fast-growing grain, permitted to grow up to about three inches. Tall long-standing grasses such as alfalfa should be avoided, since the organisms prefer dark, oxygen-poor surroundings. Rapid growth in the rotation pens should be promoted by heavy application of acid fertilizers such as ammonium sulphate, because the organism prefers an alkaline environment, such as produced by liming.

LARGE VIRAL DISEASES

Under this heading two conditions should be mentioned which are of indirect importance.

Air sac infection is a poorly defined but economically important disease of young chickens, turkeys, pigeons and pheasants. It is related to chronic respiratory disease of adult chickens and sinusitis of turkeys, thereby pointing up possible interspecies

Virologic examination being performed to determine the presence of viruses

transmission. It is believed to be caused by a pleuropneumonia-like organism. The prototype of these organisms is known as the cause of a severe infectious pneumonia in cattle, now extinct in the United States, but still prevalent in Africa, Asia and Australia.

In pheasants the disease induces primarily swellings in the head region, but it may affect the internal organs with deposition of yellow exudate on the air sacs. Symptoms are essentially respiratory in character. The available evidence suggests that the disease is transmitted through the egg, like pullorum disease. Its importance lies in the fact that pheasants may act as a source of infection for chickens and turkeys, or vice versa. Emergency treatment of individual mature pheasants might be tried by injection of terramycin (50 milligrams in mineral oil) or dihydrostreptomycin (100 milligrams per bird) into the neck or thigh region, respectively. If brooder house mortality is suspected to be caused by this disease, 200 grams per ton of aureomycin or terramycin in the feed might be helpful.

Parrot fever, psittacosis or ornithosis, is caused by *Miyagawanella psittaci*. The disease affects a variety of birds, parrots and other psittacine birds, fulmars, finches, canaries and budgerigars; it has also been found occasionally in chickens, turkeys, pigeons, ducks and pheasants. Although severe outbreaks have been seen in aviaries, particularly those receiving overseas shipments, the disease in birds is usually chronic and relatively mild. It may be accompanied by diarrhea and enlargement of the spleen. Definite diagnosis is a laboratory procedure. People may acquire the infection from inhalation of organisims in dried feces or urine or from handling infected carcasses and come down with a form of atypical pneumonia.

Cases have been reported of illness that is rather transient among pheasants yet causes ornithosis in the pheasants' caretakers. There is also suggestive evidence that some cases of air sac infection are caused by ornithosis, rather than a pleuropneumonia-like agent. Thus, the principal importance of ornithosis in pheasants lies in its potential hazard to man. Known affected birds should be destroyed or fed high levels of aureomycin (400 to 600 grams per ton) for three or more weeks in order to render them noninfectious.

VIRAL DISEASES

Of four major virus-caused pheasant diseases, two induce primarily respiratory and the other two paralytic signs.

Newcastle disease affects all domesticated and some wild birds, with pheasants no exception. In man the disease may cause a mild to severe inflammation of the eyelids (conjunctivitis). The disease was first observed as a devastating plague in the East Indies and in the British town of Newcastle on Tynne, whence it received its name. Since about 1945 the American disease has spread in somewhat milder form to every state of the Union and now constitutes a most formidable problem of the modern poultry industry. The signs are respiratory in nature, with discharge from eyes and nostrils followed by nervous signs in the form of jerking or twisting of the neck, so-called "down-benders" and "star gazers." Egg production goes rapidly downhill, the few eggs laid being bleached and soft-shelled. Mortality rate may be high, particularly in the brooder house. On postmortem examination thin yellow exudate on the air sacs is suggestive of the disease.

In pheasants the disease is relatively uncommon and mild. Chicks from parent stock either naturally or artifically exposed to the disease obtain some protection for about two weeks from passive immune bodies in the embryonic yolk. Preventive vaccination is advisable in highly congested poultry areas, especially on the basis of past experience; this should be done with commercial live virus wing-web vaccine at the age of about eight weeks. It is important to prevent prior exposure by quarantine measures.

Infectious laryngotracheitis is the other respiratory disease to which only chickens and pheasants and their crosses are susceptible. The disease is most serious in grown birds and brings about severe gasping and nasal and conjunctival discharge, accompanied by bloody or pus-like exudate in the windpipe. Death is caused by suffocation. Recovered birds may be virus carriers for life and the source of infection for new broods.

In young pheasants the disease may be indistinguishable from a severe cold, but responsible for poor growth and for unexplained mortality. In old birds egg production drops precipitously. If the diagnosis is definitely established, the old birds should be eliminated, when economically feasible, and the chicks vaccinated at the age of eight weeks in the cloaca with commercial laryngotracheitis vaccine even if the pheasant shows no symptoms.

Fowl paralysis or neural lymphomatosis is the equivalent of the corresponding disease in chickens. Growing pheasants may present droopy wings or partially paralyzed, often dragging, legs, usually on one side. On opening, the sciatic nerves may appear swollen. The incidence is rarely high. Affected birds should be culled.

Eastern equine encephalomyelitis or horse sleeping sickness is a usually fatal nervous disease of horses, pheasants and man. Other birds may become infected with the virus but are not known to

Histologic examination, done to search out minute tissue changes

show clinical evidence. The pheasant disease has been observed so far in five northeastern states. The disease is believed to be transmitted by mosquitoes and perhaps other bloodsucking insects.

In pheasants the disease tends to occur in the late summer and early fall, rarely after a killing frost. It often singles out certain pens, leaving adjacent units untouched. The signs are nervous in character and vary from incoordination and impaired flight to convulsions and prostration. No tissue changes can be detected except by microscopic examination of the brain. The handling of infected pheasants with bare hands must be considered dangerous to human health. Known affected birds should be destroyed on a pen-basis. In areas with a history of recurrent trouble, preventive vaccination during early summer with commercial equine encephalomyelitis vaccine, about one-half ml. per bird, may be considered. The vaccine is chemically killed and therefore harmless.

Work in Connecticut (*American Journal of Hygiene*, Jan. 1958) has shown that the virus may linger in the marrow of feather quills and thus become infective by feather picking. Any measure which decreases cannibalism (such as extra space, moving to new ground, protein-rich feed, anti-peck sprays and, especially, debeaking at the beginning of an outbreak) may decrease pen-mortality. An additional measure would be control of mosquitoes and of sparrows in the immediate vicinity of the pheasant pens.

Stocking and Winter Feeding of Pheasants

The true pheasants or game pheasants belong to a genus containing many species; they are designated "game" because of their extensive range in the wild state. They have become naturalized in many sections of the world, found from the Caucausus to Japan. Although of primary interest to sportsmen, they are raised by many aviaries and extensively commercially. The best known and commonest species, therefore those of the greatest interest to groups attempting propagation in most parts of the country, are the Chinese Ringneck, the Mongolian, the Blackneck, the Formosan, and the Melanistic Mutant.

STOCKING

If maximum results are to be gotten from a propagation program, it is best that all birds be stocked in cover that best meets their requirements. Suitable cover includes dense thickets of brush, grass or weeds. It is most important that all areas stocked have an abundance of cover that will provide shelter during the winter, and also some winter feed if possible; the cover should be next to some type of easily accessible winter feed.

Birds should be transported to the stocking area in a well-ventilated crate, padded on the top to prevent injury to the birds' heads. In catching the birds for crating, a landing net may be used, taking care not to injure the birds.

It is advisable to erect a feeding hopper and to supply a quantity of feed that will give the birds a chance to accustom themselves to the natural food supply. The establishing of a feeding hopper also tends to simplify selection of winter feeding stations, as in most cases birds will frequent this hopper, so a winter feeding program can follow through as soon as cold weather sets in.

In releasing pheasants from a crate, do not open the slot on the crate until the birds have had time to settle down. Do not try to handle the birds, but let them wander away by themselves. The less they are disturbed, the more likely they will stay in the cover next to where they were released.

WINTER FEEDING

States carrying on a stocking program, and those areas in which there is a large population of game pheasants, must have the co-operation of farmers, sportsmen and other interested individuals if an extensive and efficient winter feeding program is to get bests results.

Feeding stations should be set up early so that the birds will know their location and won't have trouble finding a supply of feed just before heavy snow or sleet storms. There are several excellent types of feeding stations, including standing or shocked corn (maize), hoppers protected by lean-to or tepee shelters and

Game pheasants in winter holding quarters

pole racks with ears of corn jabbed on spikes driven through the poles from the underside.

It is necessary that the stations be next to good cover and that they be built in locations giving maximum protection from drifting snow. The ordinary feeding mixture is two parts whole shelled corn to one part wheat. Some keepers prefer to add to this a percentage of buckwheat. Two percent of ordinary poultry grit should be added to the ration.

Feeding hoppers may be made of any size, with either one or two feeding sides. A wire basket made of two-inch mesh poultry netting is a good method of feeding ear corn. It can be fastened to a tree or post to prevent its tipping and being covered with snow.

A lot of experimental work has been done with food patch planting in recent years. Various grains have been used, and it is believed at the present time that standing corn is the most reliable all-around type of food patch. Buckwheat also serves as an excellent type, but it is of very little help in regions having heavy snow. Some of the sorghums are good, especially during dry seasons, but because almost as good soil and as much cultivation is required to insure a good crop of sorghum, corn is recommended. While corn may be left standing, it is necessary that buckwheat be cut and bundled and fed on racks of poles above the snow level.

The success of a feeding program depends in great part upon its being started early enough to insure available food for the birds before they are actually in need of it. Food patches furnish such a supply. Many areas cannot depend entirely upon them, but during the average winter in even the northern sections, they will simplify winter feeding to a great extent.

Swinhoe's Pheasant *(Lophura swinhoei)*

Pheasants on Shooting Preserves

A shooting preserve is an acreage either privately owned or leased on which artificially propagated game, such as Ringnecked Pheasants, is released for hunting, usually for a fee, over an extended period designated by the state game department.

New York was the first state to pass a shooting preserve law (in 1910). Since then, many more states have followed with permissive legislation.

The concept of shooting preserves is rather simple. One substitutes the incubator, brooder house and holding pen for nesting and rearing cover in the wild. This makes it possible to rear a large number of game birds on a few acres with a minimum of natural losses. The only cover type that is essential on shooting preserves is holding cover during the fall and winter months.

The recent increase in the popularity of shooting preserves is largely the result of an expanding and shifting human population. Further, the percentage of our population living in urban or metropolitan areas is increasing, with most of the population living in such areas. This means we have large centers of human population with restricted hunting opportunities. Shooting preserves, with their ability to produce large numbers of birds under artificial conditions on a few acres, are providing an answer to this critical problem.

The mechanization of game propagation, the improvement and control of quality game feed, as well as the development of effective medication for various game diseases, all have contributed to the production of game at a lower cost per bird in spite of a rise in our general economy. Artificial propagation of game a few years ago was an arduous task, requiring the use of bantam hens and a constant fight with game diseases. Thanks to the poultry industry, these barriers have been largely removed, and game can now be reared in quantity at a reasonable cost.

There are basically two types of shooting preserves, one public and the other private. If the shooting preserve is open to the general public on a daily fee basis, it is considered to be a public shooting preserve. If the clientele is restricted in any manner, the shooting preserve is called private.

One cannot help but be impressed by the rapid expansion of the shooting preserve concept that has taken place during the past few years. Certainly, shooting preserves will furnish a lot of our farm-game hunting near metropolitan areas. In time, better techniques will be developed for the flighting of various game birds, and we can look to an increase of quality and naturalness in field shooting.

The ideal terrain for a shooting preserve is gently rolling land, which does not have to be of high fertility. The size of the area varies somewhat with terrain and distribution of natural cover thereon. An area of from 300 to 500 tillable acres is sufficient. At our farm the average shooting course, where four may hunt, is approximately 30 to 40 acres. However, buffer acreage must be available between shooting courses in order to avoid conflict between hunting parties. Woody cover, especially timber, is not desirable, and the potential operator should avoid purchasing or leasing such tracts of land.

Presently the most popular game species on shooting preserves are the Ringnecked Pheasant, the Mallard Duck, the Bobwhite Quail and the Chukar. All of these species need special techniques and handling. We shall discuss only the Ringnecked Pheasant.

The Ringnecked Pheasant is considered to be the most popular game bird on shooting preserves. This grand game bird has the unique ability of reverting to the wild within a few minutes after being released, which delights both hunter and preserve operator.

A full-plumage, strong-flying bird with the conformation of the Ringnecked Pheasant is needed on the preserve. Pheasants with bobtails and/or bare backs, an evidence of cannibalism, should not be released. These birds show poor management and are looked upon disdainfully by the average sportsman. Ample space, twenty to twenty-five square feet per bird in holding pens, is the best assurance against cannibalism. Debeaking, plant cover, feed, etc.,

Good field dogs are essential to the success of a shooting preserve

are some of the other management tools employed in controlling cannibalism—one of the most important problems in the game industry.

Pheasants may be released in the field by different techniques. However, inasmuch as the percentage of return is important for stipulate that the birds be full-plumaged, 16 weeks or more of age and of a given sex ratio.

Some operators seem to prefer pheasants that are predominately Chinese, whereas others prefer a bird that is mostly Mongolian. A "shooting preserve pheasant" still needs to be developed. It is rather doubtful that all operators will agree on the genetic composition of such a pheasant, but the possibilities should be investigated.

The most desirable pheasant is one that has not been handicapped by being brailed or by shearing its flight feathers (primaries). However, brailed birds will recover and be satisfactory flyers, providing they have sufficient time to exercise their wing muscles in a

English Blackneck Pheasant *(Phasianus colchicus septentrionalis)*

large holding pen, which should be approximately seven feet high, 150 feet long, and 100 feet wide.

Pheasants may be released in the field by different techniques. However, inasmuch as the precentage of return is important for the profitable management of a shooting preserve, it is recommended that pheasants be released less than an hour before the hunting parties enter the field. It is unnecessary and extremely costly to release birds several days or more prior to actual hunting, for the birds would soon disperse over the countryside and would be a loss to the operator.

The recovery rate of pheasants by hunters on a preserve should be about seventy percent of the birds released. Releasing pheasants thirty to sixty minutes ahead of the hunters either singly or in small groups in good cover is the best known method to recover a high percentage of the released birds and to assure natural field shooting.

The release technique that has been most satisfactory is to rock the birds just sufficiently so that they might be placed in natural cover without taking flight. A bird is rocked by placing its head under a wing and then swinging the bird back and forth in a half circle. The amount of rocking is an art. It is possible to rock birds to such an extent that they will not give a satisfactory field performance when found by the hunting party.

One of the important management features on a shooting preserve is manipulation of holding or release cover throughout the season. Cover that may provide excellent release sites in early fall may be flattened in late winter by snow. The ideal cover will have to be developed within the various climatic areas throughout the country. A fairly dense herbaceous cover up to two or three feet above the ground needs to be developed so that it will hold pheasants until they are flushed by the hunting parties. If the cover is thin, the pheasants may take flight or run ahead of the dogs when the party enters the shooting course. Up to the present time, food plots of one-eighth to one-half acre in size are most desirable as release covers. It is suggested that one of these plots be planted for every three to four acres on a shooting course.

In the fall, shortly before the shooting season, stopping strips twenty to thirty feet in width are mowed around release sites, such as food plots or natural cover. The use of this technique tends to hold the birds within the plant cover near the place of their release. When the pheasant approaches the stopping strip on foot, the bird hesitates to leave the comparative security of the plant cover at the release site and is inclined to turn back.

Food plots are usually made up of grain sorghum with amber cane, atlas sorghum, kaffir and sudan grass and are broadcast or drilled in seven-inch rows at the rate of about twelve pounds an acre. These plots usually grow eight to ten feet in height, especially during summers with normal rainfall, and are sometimes undesirable for early season hunting. The dwarf hybrid or combine sorghums furnish satisfactory cover during the early part of the season. For varieties adapted to particular areas, seeding rates, etc., one should consult state agricultural college extension personnel or the county agent to make sure he has the suitable variety of sorghum and the proper cultural practices for his soil and climatic conditions.

Good dogs are essential in the successful management of a preserve. Most new preserve operators neglect this phase of management and underrate the value of top quality hunting dogs. Good bird dogs may well spell the difference between profit and loss at the end of the season. Pointing dogs furnish fully half of the enjoyment of hunters.

The ideal preserve dog is one that has some qualities that are desired in a field trial dog with the exception of ranging. Wide-ranging bird dogs have a tendency to miss pheasants that have been planted on the course and sometimes are instrumental in flushing the birds before the hunting party can get into shooting position. A preserve dog should be trained to range rather close, to be staunch to shot and to retrieve without undue handling by the guide. Even style is important. There is quite a bit of satisfaction to both the operator and hunter in watching the dog on a stylish point.

Certainly it is difficult to distinguish between the importance of high quality game birds, natural cover and top quality field dogs, as they are all necessary in the operation of a preserve to guarantee repeat business.

Our hunting technique is based on providing a well trained bird dog and guide for each group of four hunters. The guide directs

180

Part of the pleasure of a good shooting preserve is a well-trained dog.
This spaniel retrieves to hand

the party over the shooting course in a line, which contracts or expands as the hunting course narrows or widens.

A white jacket is worn by all hunters. These slip-on garments are like the ordinary button-type windbreaker, but are sleeveless and large enough to be worn over regular clothing in cold weather. These white jackets identify hunters on a shooting course to farm personnel and assist members of a hunting pary in locating each other. However, these jackets aren't effective when the ground is covered with snow.

Advertising is just as necessary in managing a shooting preserve as in any other private enterprise. One should not expect customers to appear automatically; they have to be encouraged. Newspapers, radio, and TV are all means of reaching potential customers and informing them of the facilities offered at your preserve.

Once the hunter has arrived at the preserve, every consideration should be given to his safety and comfort. Such apparent incidentals as a warm welcome and comfortable surroundings all tend to make satisfied customers. Safety should be stressed prior to field shooting to avoid any embarrassment to the guests. Facilities for the cleaning and freezing of pheasants are desirable and should be made available at a reasonable cost.

The hunter expects the best field sport possible. He wants his hunting as natural as possible—not too tough, but a happy medium. He wants a day of outdoor thrills and above all he should not be hurried or pushed. Give him ample time to enjoy the hunting, the dogs and his natural surroundings.

Some preserves fully expect an annual repeat business of 90 percent of their former customers. Anything less than this should be a warning sight to the preserve operator.

There are two basic methods for charging for hunting on a preserve. One is based on the number of birds released and the other on the number of birds harvested. Both of these techniques have certain merits. The successful operator is one who charges a fair price for services rendered.

APPENDIX I

Suspected Pheasant Diseases According to Main Symptom

DIARRHEA
Navel ill
Pullorum Dis.
Fowl typhoid
*Paratyphoid
Fowl cholera
*Ornithosis

RESPIRATORY DISTRESS
Gapeworm Disease
Newcastle Disease
Laryngotracheitis
Aspergillosis
Air sac infection

PARALYSIS
Injury
Botulism
*Equ. encephalomyelitis
Fowl paralysis
Muscular dystrophy
Fowl cholera

EMACIATION
Moniliasis
Asperillosis
Tuberculosis

*Potentially dangerous to man

APPENDIX II

Days Required To Hatch Eggs Of Common Pheasant Species

Species	Days
Amherst's Pheasant	23-24
Bel's Pheasant	26-27
Black-necked	24-25
Cheer	27-28
Chinese Ringneck	24-25
Eared Pheasants	
Blue	27-28
Brown (Manchurian)	27-28
Edwards's Pheasant	24-25
Firebacks	24-25
Formosan	24-25
Golden	23-24
Golden, Dark-Throated	23-24
Imperial	24-25
Impeyan	27-28
Kalij, Black-backed	24-25
Kalij, Lineated	26-27
Kalij, Nepal	24-25
Kalij, White-crested	24-25
Melanistic Mutant	24-25
Mikado	27-28
Mongolian	24-25
Reeve's Pheasant	24-25
Silver	26-27
Swinhoe's Pheasant	24-25
Tragopans	27-28

Index

A complete index of illustrations can be found on succeeding pages following the index of subject matter.

Illustrations Index

Frontis (Chinese Ringneck Pheasant)